THE GREAT PONY MYSTERY

In the same series

PONY PAGEANT
Sylvia Scott-White

PONY WATCH
Elinore Havers

A PONY TO CATCH
Elinore Havers

PONY SLEUTHS
Elinore Havers

GREY ARROW
Catherine Carey

ONLY ONE PONY
Elinore Havers

LITTLE GREY PONY
Hilda Boden

Other pony stories by Elinore Havers appear in the companion series, Crown Pony Hardbacks

THE GREAT PONY MYSTERY

by

ELINORE HAVERS

LUTTERWORTH PRESS
GUILDFORD AND LONDON

First published 1969

This paperback edition first published 1975

The Publishers are grateful to Miss J. Kemp, Mounters Farm, Chawton, Hants, for permission to take the cover photograph at her riding stable

ISBN 0 7188 2224 2

PRINTED OFFSET LITHO AND BOUND IN GREAT BRITAIN
BY COX & WYMAN LTD
LONDON, FAKENHAM AND READING

CONTENTS

CHAPTER ONE

"AN ILL WIND"

When Mrs. Manning said they wouldn't be able to have a summer holiday Debbie and Jonathan pretended they didn't mind.

Their father had died several years ago and they now lived in a small cottage. They had come to like it, especially as a large paddock went with it so they were able to keep their ponies, Kit-Kat and Puck. Their mother said the ponies were their only extravagance and people must have some fun. Debbie sometimes thought that her mother didn't have much fun though she was good at arranging it for her and Jonathan.

At any rate, if they didn't go away for a holiday she needn't worry over leaving the ponies and her other animals. It was rather sickening though, when everyone else was going away—some were even going abroad—and they'd all talk about where they'd been when they met next term.

Mrs. Manning worked part-time at a nearby girls' boarding school so she had the same holidays as Debbie and Jonathan, who went to the grammar school in Chelsdon, their nearest town.

It was during the first week of the summer holidays that she said she must go over to the school to fetch some books. Debbie and Jonathan went with her in their small, and old, car, Jonathan in front with Mrs. Manning and Debbie in the back with Tiger, their Boxer. The school was closed, it looked deserted and rather lonely, Debbie thought. They stayed in the car while their mother went inside.

"Rather decent playing fields they've got," said Jonathan.

"The swimming pool's smashing," Debbie told him.

"I wish we could've gone to the sea," he said. He liked swimming almost better than anything.

"I don't much mind, there'll be Pony Club rallies and there may be a gymkhana near enough to go to," said Debbie, playing with Tiger's ears. He was sprawling on the back seat and leaving her very little room.

"Shall we go back by the common and give Tiger a run?" Mrs. Manning asked, coming back with a bundle of books under her arm and getting into the driving seat.

"Oh do, Mummie, he's squashing me horribly," said Debbie, and Jonathan pointed out that a run wouldn't make him any smaller. "We can stretch our legs," Debbie said.

The road to the common was narrow and twisting. Rounding a bend they met a caravan and Mrs. Manning stopped. It was painted blue with red wheels and was drawn by an enormous bay horse.

"Gypsies!" said Debbie.

"I think they're holiday-makers," Mrs. Manning said. "I'll have to reverse, they can't back easily." She leaned out and called "I'll go back."

A woman was leading the horse and she stared

at Mrs. Manning and then cried, "Diana Manning!"

"Rosemary!" exclaimed Mrs. Manning. She switched off the engine and jumped out. "Fancy seeing you after all this time! Were you coming to visit us?"

"Do you live here? I didn't know." Mrs. Fraser sounded tired. Debbie wondered if she'd walked all day leading the horse, and if she was alone.

"Are you having a caravanning holiday?" Mrs. Manning asked. "It must be tremendous fun."

"It ought to be but it hasn't been for us," said Mrs. Fraser. "Everything's gone wrong."

"I am sorry," Mrs. Manning said. "Anything we can do to help? Aren't the children with you? They're about the same age as my two, if I remember rightly."

"That's just it," Mrs. Fraser said sadly. "We only started three days ago and yesterday morning Elizabeth got tonsilitis and had to go into hospital."

"Oh, how wretched for her," Mrs. Manning said.

"That's not all. Last night Ian got on the roof of the caravan, goodness knows why, and fell off and broke his arm."

"Oh, my dear, how dreadful," said Mrs. Manning sympathetically.

"Mummie," said Jonathan, "we ought to move before something comes along and wants to get by."

"Of course," agreed Mrs. Manning. "I'll go back and find somewhere to stop and you can tell us everything." She began to back slowly and the caravan followed them.

"Lucky you're good at reversing," Jonathan said.

"Daddy taught me. He said one was so helpless if one couldn't reverse efficiently. This is a safe place to stop for a chat." Mrs. Manning drew up on a triangle of grass where the road forked.

"It looks a smashing caravan," Debbie said as Mrs. Fraser stopped near them. "Miles nicer to drive a horse than be towed behind a car."

"I haven't seen Mrs. Fraser for years," Mrs. Manning explained as they got out of the car. "We were at school together and we kept up for a long time before we lost touch. How disappointing for them to have their holiday go wrong. Those poor children!"

"At least they're both in the same hospital!" said Mrs. Fraser as they joined her. She smiled faintly. "Now I'm taking the caravan back to where we hired it as quickly as possible, as I want to get back to the children, only one can't hurry."

"How can we help?" Mrs. Manning asked. "Come and stay the night with us? It's only a couple of miles. Do."

"That'd be lovely if it's not giving you trouble? The caravan's got me down, without the kids it's no fun."

"Of course you must come," Mrs. Manning said firmly. "And I've got an idea—could we take the caravan back for you? Then you could go straight to the children tomorrow."

"It'd be marvellous. Please take it over for the rest of the time. Ian's having his arm set and it'll be rather wretched for him so I'd like to be there.

Only I'm sure you don't want to be burdened with a caravan?"

"We'll enjoy it," Mrs. Manning said. "Shan't we?"

"Rather," said Debbie, "smashing!"

"Super, as good as camping, better in fact," said Jonathan.

"If you're sure——" Mrs. Fraser said. "It'd be a great help to me. It's a nice caravan, very well-equipped, we hired it through some friends. The owners don't let it out to just anyone and they use it themselves."

"It'll be a treat for us," Mrs. Manning told her, "as we are doing without a summer holiday this year. Just tell us where it's got to be taken, and the date it must be there, and we'll get it there. Of course I'll pay for our share."

Mrs. Fraser wouldn't hear of this, they were doing her a great favour in taking charge of it, but Mrs. Manning could buy the provisions she'd laid in. "Lots of tinned food in case we were out of reach of shops."

"And a holiday from cooking!" Mrs. Manning said. "Now, I'll go home and get tea ready and Jonathan can show you the way. Perhaps you can teach him about managing a horse and caravan."

Debbie said she'd walk with them because it would be exercise for Tiger, so their mother went on, leaving them to follow.

Tea was ready by the time they arrived, and when she went out she found Mrs. Fraser giving the children a lesson in taking the horse out of the shafts and then unharnessing him. After this they introduced him—his name was Ajax—to the ponies, and as they seemed to get on all right he was turned out in the paddock. He rolled and then began to graze. Mrs. Fraser told them he was very quiet and a good worker.

While they had tea they made plans. There were ten days before they had to return the caravan. Jonathan went to get maps. Mrs. Fraser advised them to avoid main roads and steep hills. "Luckily it's fairly flat round here and there aren't many towns."

"What about the ponies?" asked Jonathan who was lying on the floor eating cake and studying a map he'd spread out. "Couldn't it be a riding tour too?"

"They'd be useful," Mrs. Fraser said. "Sometimes we stopped for the night away from a village and when we wanted something someone had to walk."

"It would be marvellous to take them," Debbie said, and then she exclaimed, "my animals!"

"Oh dear, yes, your pets," Mrs. Manning said.

"You can't take your zoo," said Jonathan.

Debbie's collection of animals seldom numbered less than a dozen, if one died (or escaped) she'd take in a stray and care for it, or be given a homeless, and sometimes ailing, little creature.

At the moment the shed in the garden housed several rabbits, Wiggs the hedgehog, Hammish the hamster (he was Scottish but that was how he liked his name pronounced) and a new family of guinea-pigs. Three bantams lived in a little run made by Jonathan. The cock was called Henry and the hens

Catherine of Aragon and Anne Boleyn. Debbie was saving up for the rest of his wives. Snoozy the dormouse was asleep in a cardboard box in her hanky and glove drawer.

"Could Tim Bristow look after them?" Mrs. Manning suggested, and Debbie's face lost its worried look.

"Yes, he'd be all right. I wouldn't let anyone else."

"Let him!" snorted Jonathan. "Jolly good of him, if he'll take it on."

Tim Bristow was the Rector's son and a keen naturalist. "Of course he will," said Debbie. "He's got three grass snakes and two lizards and a white rat. He'll be pleased to have some more animals even if it's only for a few days. I can take Snoozy," she added. "He can live in my pocket most of the time and have his box at night. As long as we can keep Tiger from finding him."

Her mother sighed. She could happily have done without Snoozy, guarding him from Tiger and the two cats was an ever-present worry. "How many people will the caravan hold?" she asked Mrs. Fraser.

"Four or five. There are two full-sized bunks and a shorter one. It'd be all right for Debbie. And there's a tent and two sleeping-bags."

"Four or five," Mrs. Manning said thoughtfully.

"Why, Mummie?" asked Debbie.

"It seems a pity not to share this treat with anyone. I was wondering about Lucy."

"That'd be marvellous!" Debbie exclaimed. "But would she be allowed to come?"

"I'll have to see what her mother thinks about it," Mrs. Manning said.

"Oh, I do hope she can," Debbie said.

"Same here," Jonathan put in.

"She could travel in the van and not walk much. Lucy's a friend of Debbie's," she explained to Mrs. Fraser. "Last year she had a bad illness, and although she's quite over it she mustn't do anything strenuous or get over-tired. Do you think caravanning would be too much for her?"

Mrs. Fraser thought for a minute and then said, "No, not if she's sensible about it. There's a good deal to do starting off in the morning and camping at night but quite a lot of the chores can be done sitting down, the cooking round a fire for instance."

"Spud-bashing," said Jonathan.

"All that," agreed Mrs. Fraser, "though she won't thank you if you leave all the potato peeling to her."

"Not too long a day or going late to bed," Mrs. Manning said thoughtfully, and Mrs. Fraser said they had to go to bed before it was dark because the only light was an electric torch.

"I'll run over and ask Mrs. Whitby," Mrs. Manning said. "It's easier to talk it over than to telephone. I'd like Lucy to come, she's been very patient about this year of going slow, hasn't she, Debbie?"

"Frightfully," said Debbie, who knew better than anyone else how much Lucy minded being left out of things. "She's done half the year. She crosses every day off on a calendar."

"It'll be rotten for her seeing us ride all day,"

Jonathan said. "Riding was what she liked best," he explained to Mrs. Fraser. "She had a jolly good pony."

"A grey called Cobweb," Debbie said. "But she can ride again at the end of the year, six months and a bit from now. And then she'll have a new pony."

"She must have hated parting with it," Mrs. Fraser said.

"Her parents thought it'd be so tantalizing for her to have Cobweb and not ride him," Mrs. Manning explained, "and she'd have outgrown him. So they sold him to a very good home and Lucy sees him sometimes. Jonathan, who'd you like as tent-mate? We want two boys. Mark?"

"Oh yes, let's have Mark."

"He'd be good on a caravan holiday," said their mother."

"Mark's so sensible!" chanted Jonathan and Debbie.

Their mother laughed. "Everyone says Mark's so sensible. He's a reliable sort of boy. He's a cousin and two years older than Jonathan."

"He's got two years more sense than me and I've got two years more sense than Debbie, who hasn't much anyway!"

Debbie rose up in rage and their mother said "Stop it, you two!" Then she drove off to see Lucy's mother, and Mrs. Fraser took Jonathan and Debbie to see the inside of the caravan, which they'd been longing to do.

It was exciting to put down the steps and climb up into the van where they'd be living for the next ten days. It was larger than it looked from outside and divided in two by a big curtain which was drawn back so that they could see the three bunks in the bedroom end, one on each side and a shorter one across the end. Debbie tried it and found she fitted it nicely. Gay flower-patterned covers on the bunks (which were settees by day) matched the curtains at the little windows. There were lockers under the bunks and shelves everywhere.

In the front half of the caravan there was a folding table and four folding chairs. Mrs. Fraser showed them an oil-stove in a metal-lined locker. "It's useful for cooking in a hurry but a camp-fire's the real thing. There are simply splendid cupboards." She opened the doors and they saw one full of groceries and provisions, another with a dust-pan and brush and cleaning utensils, another held saucepans and an assortment of china mugs hung on hooks in a neat row.

"I think they must collect mugs," Mrs. Fraser said, "they're all different and so attractive, and they save on washing-up, no saucers."

The tent and sleeping bags lay in a heap on the floor. Jonathan thought of Mark and himself sleeping in it and he wished they could start at once.

Underneath the caravan, at the back, a small meat-safe hung, and there was also a shovel, Ajax's nose-bag and wheel-skids for use going down steep hills.

They had just finished inspecting everything when they heard a car and their mother drove up.

"Can Lucy come?" called Debbie anxiously.

"Yes." Her mother got out and came across to the van. "Mrs. Whitby thinks it won't be tiring as long as she doesn't walk much, only up hills so as not to overwork Ajax, and there are hardly any hills round here."

"Hurrah! That's terrific!" Debbie said.

"Jolly good!" said Jonathan. "Now we want Mark."

They rang him up that evening and he was thrilled at the prospect. It was arranged he should come by train the next day and join them at midday.

"Lucky us and poor Frasers," Debbie said, "but it's an ill wind that blows nobody any good."

CHAPTER TWO

THE FIRST NIGHT

THERE was a fearful lot to do the next morning. Mrs. Fraser left early by bus to stay in Chelsdon where her children were in hospital. Mrs. Manning and Debbie sorted out the clothes they'd need and stowed them in the lockers in the caravan. Meanwhile Jonathan caught the ponies and collected grooming and tack-cleaning kit which he packed into a bucket to use for watering the ponies. Mrs. Manning transferred food from the larder to the caravan's meat-safe and cupboards.

"Mummie," said Debbie, "can I go and ask Tim to look after my animals now? And what about the cats?"

The cats were called Appy and Tite because they ate so much. They weren't really Debbie's so much as family cats, but all animals were adopted by her and became hers in the end.

"Mrs. Austin will feed them," her mother answered. "She's going to look after the cottage for us. I asked her last night and fixed up about the cats. You run and arrange with Tim to look after the others."

Debbie came back saying Tim was delighted and he had a young jackdaw. "When's Lucy coming?" she asked.

"At eleven, and I want to start then. We're picking Mark up at Witherley station at one."

"Uncle Robert only has tractors, no cart-horses, but I expect Mark can drive a horse," Debbie said. Uncle Robert was Mark's father who had a large farm about fifty miles away.

"He can drive a tractor, which is much harder," said Jonathan. "Mrs. Fraser showed me how to drive Ajax, it only needs practice."

"We'll get plenty of practice," said Mrs. Manning. "I think everything's arranged and we can start when Lucy comes."

"The animals will miss me," Debbie said mournfully. Then Mrs. Whitby and Lucy arrived and she rushed to meet them.

"Hello Deb! Isn't this super!" shouted Lucy as she got out of the car.

"It's a great surprise for us," said Mrs. Whitby. "Aren't you thrilled, Debbie? Lucy is."

"Terribly thrilled. I'm jolly glad she's coming. And Locket."

"Of course. She couldn't go without Locket," said Mrs. Whitby. Locket was a little Yorkshire terrier which had been given to Lucy to help make up for having to part with Cobweb. Her real name was Frolic—it was on her pedigree—but Lucy's father called her Locket because she and Lucy were never apart. It was rather like Frolic so she soon came to know it and they hardly ever called her anything else.

"Who's going to look after your zoo?" Lucy asked.

"Tim Bristow. And Mrs. Austin's going to feed

Appy and Tite." Appy, a tabby, was asleep in the sun in the front garden. Tite, black with white paws and shirt-front, was on the little lawn watching sparrows on the roof and, no doubt, wishing he could fly!

Lucy pointed to a suitcase in the back of their car. "This is my luggage."

"Unpack it in the caravan and leave the case indoors," said Mrs. Manning. "Jonathan will carry it for you."

He lugged it to the van, grumbling about the amount of clothes girls needed, and they all heaved to get it up thc steps. Debbie helped Lucy stow her clothes away in a locker.

The next thing was to harness Ajax and back him into the shafts. Luckily Mrs. Manning had experience in driving, "but nothing as large as this," she said. Ajax towered above them all.

"We're ready to start," she announced. "What's the matter, Deb?"

Debbie, who was looking worried, answered that it was Snoozy. She had forgotten that Locket would be in the caravan, and Locket liked mice. "I'd better take him to Tim to keep with the others," she suggested.

"Your animals!" her mother sighed. "Off you go and then catch us up."

Debbie rode off holding Snoozy's box, Jonathan mounted Kit-Kat, and Lucy said goodbye to her mother and climbed up to the driver's seat. Mrs. Manning led Ajax and the caravan trundled out of the yard. Once on the road Mrs. Manning got up beside Lucy. "I was scared of ramming the gatepost if I tried to drive out," she confessed, "it's a sharp turn and I've never driven anything as big as this. Suppose you drive, Lucy, it'll be useful if you can take over from me."

"I'd love to," Lucy said. She took the reins and Mrs. Manning gave her a driving lesson. Besides being useful to have two drivers she thought it would make up a little to Lucy for not being able to ride.

Debbie soon caught them up. Tim, she said, was more than pleased to have the opportunity of studying the habits of a dormouse. She rode on ahead with Jonathan. It was terribly exciting to ride off for ten days and not know where they were going. She hoped for at least one adventure. She little knew what was in store for them!

Locket sat between Lucy and Mrs. Manning and Tiger ran by the ponies. Jonathan's route was along lanes. This was a good idea except that the caravan almost filled a narrow lane so it was im-impossible to pass anything. They had several delays when a motorist had to back to the nearest gateway, and Mrs. Manning said they'd have to avoid narrow lanes.

"We're not going to meet Mark on time," she said, "will you two ride on to Witherley station and tell him we're coming?"

After walking at Ajax's slow pace it was nice to trot along. They reached the small wayside station as the train came in and Mark appeared carrying a kit-bag.

"Hi there!" yelled Jonathan.

"Hi Jon, hello Deb!" Mark put down his kit-bag.

"The caravan's coming. It's a super one but frightfully slow. The horse walks at about one mile an hour," explained Jonathan. "So we're behind schedule."

Presently it came in sight and they went to meet it. Lucy was driving and Mark, who had met her before, said "Hello Lucy, are you the charioteer?"

"It's quite difficult but I haven't run into anything yet. It's super fun."

"You're doing fine. You'll be a champion driver by the end of the trip," Mrs. Manning said. "I'm sorry we're late, Mark. Ajax is slower than I expected."

"Don't worry, Aunt Diana," Mark said cheerfully. "He's a massive beast and there's no hurry." He put his kit-bag in the van.

"I'm in a hurry for lunch," Jonathan grumbled. "I'm starving. It's ages since breakfast."

"We'll have it as soon as we find somewhere to stop," said his mother.

They found a grassy patch where they could pull off the road near a stream where they watered the ponies and Ajax. Then they tethered Kit-Kat and Puck to graze and gave Ajax a small feed in his nosebag; chaff and oats were carried in a locker under the driver's seat.

While they had a picnic lunch Jonathan and Mark looked at the map and planned a new route.

"How many miles a day, Aunt Diana?" asked Mark.

"Ten, perhaps twelve if it's flat country. Ajax is a slow walker, and the caravan's too heavy to expect him to trot much."

"And everything rattles like mad if he trots," Lucy said. "We tried for a little way."

"We must leave time to find a camping site at night," Mrs. Manning said, "and we've supper to cook. We'll have a cold snack at midday and cook at night."

"It doesn't matter where we go," said Lucy. "It's more fun to just go anywhere and see where we get to and what happens."

But Jonathan and Mark thought this was a slack way of touring, and they made out a new route avoiding towns, steep hills, narrow lanes or main roads.

They allowed Ajax time to digest his feed and then harnessed up and went on until about four o'clock, when Mrs. Manning decided it was time to look for a camping site.

"Shall Mark and I go on and ask at a farm?" suggested Jonathan.

Debbie had given Puck to Mark, and she was walking with Lucy, who was giving Locket a run.

Mrs. Manning thought this a good idea. "Yes, do. Be sure and say we only want to stay one night. We'll want to buy milk and we need grazing for the horses."

The boys rode on ahead at a spanking trot and Lucy and Debbie walked beside Ajax talking about the pony Lucy would have when she was able to ride again. They had decided on a bright bay with black mane and tail (long, of course), not a grey in case he was a disappointment after Cobweb. They'd chosen several names so as to get one that suited him when they saw Jonathan and Mark riding back towards them.

"No go," Mark said, pulling up. He pointed towards a farm near the road. "They won't have campers at any price."

"Oh dear, I hope all the farmers don't feel like that," Mrs. Manning said. "We must just keep trying."

"There's another farm on the other side of the road, just a little way on," Jonathan said. "Let's ask there."

"Be sure and say we won't do any damage or leave litter," Mrs. Manning said.

"I should think not, we aren't beastly litter louts," Lucy said.

"Okay," Jonathan said and they trotted off again.

Soon they were back with the same tale. No campers.

"I hope they haven't had some bad campers who've put them off letting people camp," Mrs. Manning said. She looked at her watch. "It's getting late and we're sure to take rather a long time to make camp and cook our supper the first night—we must find somewhere soon. Perhaps I'd better ask at the next farm, they may not realize you have a grown-up with you. If we've no luck we must stop at the first wide stretch of grass by the road. Or we might come to a common. I believe the police move you on after twenty-four hours but we wouldn't want to stay that long."

Police! Moved on! It sounded horrid. Debbie had wanted an adventure but not one with the police moving them on.

"I'm jolly hungry," Jonathan complained. They had decided to miss tea and to have a cooked supper at six.

"It must be like this for gypsies," Lucy said, "having nowhere to stop."

"Cheer up!" Mrs. Manning said, "there's a farm just ahead, in those trees on the left, maybe our luck will change."

They reached the entrance and she gave Lucy Ajax's reins. "Keep your fingers crossed!"

"*Make* them let us camp," said Jonathan.

"Implore and entreat and beseech them!" Lucy said.

"Go on your bended knees, Mummie," said Debbie earnestly. It really was serious—nowhere to sleep.

"I'll do all that," Mrs. Manning said with a laugh, though she was feeling very worried, for she hadn't expected things to turn out like this.

When she came back she was smiling and the waiting children knew it was all right. "A nice farmer and a very nice farm, a field for Ajax and the ponies and a good site for us. We're in luck this time."

The farmer showed them where to go and the caravan rocked and swayed across the grass with no sound except the creak of harness and a rattle of crockery.

"Not under the trees," Mrs. Manning said, "they're elms which are apt to drop boughs suddenly, besides if there was a thunderstorm in the night under a tree would be a bad place."

"It won't thunder tonight," the farmer assured her.

They turned out Ajax and the ponies. Tiger sprawled in the shade, tired after the day's march, and Locket pranced round exploring.

"What'll we do first?" asked Mark. "The fire?"

"As it's late perhaps we'd better use the stove——" Mrs. Manning began, but they interrupted her. "A camp fire. A fire's the real thing."

"Very well," Mrs. Manning agreed. "You boys light it. Debbie, will you fetch water and some milk? The farmer said he'd supply us and there's a big milk-can in one of the cupboards. Lucy and I will make beds."

Everyone worked fast. The boys were lucky in finding dry sticks and they soon had a fire going. Lucy cooked sausages and bacon while Mrs. Manning and Debbie spread ground-sheets to sit on and brought out plates and cutlery. The mugs hanging on a shelf in the caravan were rather fun as they were all different. Debbie chose one with a huntsman on it for Lucy, and a blue one with Scottie terriers for herself, for her mother she chose one with primroses. Jonathan's had pictures of old cars and Mark's was red with yellow squiggles. There were still three left, all different too.

The boys put up the tent, not without some difficulty and a good deal of laughter, for they couldn't find out how it should go and the first time they got it up it collapsed on top of them.

The sun was dipping behind the trees when they sat down to supper, the air was warm and still and there was a gold haze in the distance. Never had sausages tasted so delicious.

"We mustn't be so late again," Mrs. Manning said. "It'll be dark before we've washed up and washed ourselves. Not tired, Lucy, I hope?"

"No," Lucy answered fiercely, for she hated being reminded about it. "I mean, no thank you, Aunt Diana," (she called Mrs. Manning this though they were not related). "I'm fine. It's been a super day and Locket's loved it."

"Ten whole days of it," Debbie said happily.

"A nice lot of days to cross off my calendar when I get home," Lucy said.

They were finishing with fruit salad when the farmer's wife arrived to ask if there was anything they needed.

"How kind of you," Mrs. Manning said. "We've everything, thank you."

"And you'll really sleep out here?" she asked. "Rather you than me!"

"This is our first night," Debbie told her. "It'll be smashing."

"You'll have colds by morning, and sore throats too, I shouldn't wonder. And the spiders!"

"We'll tell you about it in the morning," Lucy promised.

It was almost dark before they finished washing up and the hot water ran out, so the boys washed very skimpily in cold before snuggling into their sleeping bags with Tiger between them.

Debbie and Lucy lay in bed with Locket beside Lucy, listening to Mrs. Manning moving about as she tidied up by the light of a torch. There were other sounds too, a cow lowing in the distance and a dog barking, rustlings in the grass and then an owl hooted. Very soon they both slept soundly. But Tiger and Locket only dozed all night. Each thought he—or she—was responsible for guarding the camp.

CHAPTER THREE

TROUBLE ON BILBERRY DOWN

DEBBIE woke to hear the crackle of dry sticks. The boys were up and had lit the fire. Soon a most delicious smell of frying bacon crept into the caravan, making its inmates hurry with their dressing.

Breakfast was cornflakes followed by eggs and bacon. The tea had a pleasant smoky taste from the wood-fire. When they had finished Lucy and Debbie went to fetch water for washing-up from the farm, and they assured the farmer's wife that they hadn't caught colds or got sore throats, but they were sure she didn't believe them. Nor that they hadn't seen any spiders.

"Actually, I did have a earwig in my bed," Debbie said as they walked back. "It was rather sweet!"

When they had packed up they looked round to see that nothing was left out. There was only a flattened circle of grass and a little black patch where the fire had been.

"I don't like that," said Mrs. Manning. "If we take up the turf with our shovel and then put it back when we go we'll avoid marking the grass. If we water it the turf won't die."

They thanked the farmer and paid him, and then Ajax threw his weight into his collar and the caravan moved forward, swaying and creaking over the grass and out onto the road. Another day of exploration had begun. With a night behind them they felt like veteran campers.

"Where are we going today, Mummie?" Debbie asked, trotting Puck up beside the caravan.

"You must ask the route-planners," her mother replied, and called to Mark. "Where are we making for?"

"Bilberry Down. It looks as if it's a good big stretch of downland where the riders could go across and meet the caravan at the far side."

"That's a good idea," Mrs. Manning approved. "I'll pack you some lunch and you can picnic. Take the ponies' tether ropes."

Lucy drove while Mrs. Manning cut sandwiches and packed them in a haversack which Jonathan slung over his shoulder. Then he took another look at the map and arranged where the riders should meet the caravan.

"Four o'clock," Mark suggested. "Ajax won't get us there any earlier. You'll have time to spare but you can ride about and explore. And pick bilberries," he added.

Jonathan and Debbie fastened the tether ropes to their saddles by tying them to the metal Ds so that they lay across the ponies' withers. Then they turned off and went along a narrow, grassy track.

Debbie turned in her saddle to wave to Lucy who was driving, and then she said to Jonathan, "I don't know what bilberries are like."

"Small, blue-ish, and they grow on little short

bushes a bit like heather only different leaves."

"Well, I'm glad you know, because I'm not eating any berries I'm not certain aren't poisonous," Debbie stated. "I say, this is fun, camping and riding about."

"Smashing," Jonathan agreed.

Then the track dwindled into a narrow path and Debbie pulled Puck back behind Kit-Kat who always wanted to be in front. It went up hill between high hedges and tall bracken which brushed their knees.

Soon they reached a gate, and Jonathan said, "Bags open it. I simply must get Kit-Kat better at gates."

So Debbie sat and watched while Jonathan struggled to get Kit-Kat up to the gate and then to prevent him backing away before he could open it. It opened towards them, which is difficult on an unwilling pony.

"Do let me," she said at last. Puck was good at gates. He was a red roan with a perfect temperament, remaining steady whatever happened and always willing to do his best.

"Kit-Kat *must* now I've started," Jonathan said, red in the face but persevering.

He used his legs strenuously to keep Kit-Kat up to the gate and managed to open it. Kit-Kat backed away rapidly, but Jonathan hung on and made him stand while Debbie rode through.

"There, you see. He just needs practice." He pulled the gate shut and made Kit-Kat wait while he made sure it was latched. "What a marvellous place to ride!" he exclaimed as he trotted up beside

Puck. "We've never been anywhere like this before. Kit-Kat'll be mad keen to gallop."

Bilberry Down stretched away in front of them, green and smooth and inviting them to gallop.

Kit-Kat snorted and began to prance sideways. Even the staid Puck danced on the short springy turf, and the children let the ponies have their heads.

They went into a fast canter which soon became a gallop and Kit-Kat went ahead. But Jonathan soon pulled up. "This beastly haversack's bumping about all the time. Let's have lunch and then it'll be empty and no trouble."

"It's rather early," Debbie objected, reining in Puck.

"It's never too early to eat," Jonathan remarked, "or too late either. The great open spaces have gone to Kit-Kat's head and he's longing to go flat out."

They unsaddled the ponies and put on their head-collars (which they carried buckled round the ponies' necks) and then tethered them to some bushes. They began to graze at once and the children sat down on the grass which was warm and smelt deliciously of thyme.

"Perfect!" Debbie said. "Except there's no water for the ponies. We must look out for a stream."

"We couldn't gallop them after drinking," Jonathan pointed out. "This short grass is just right, they can't blow themselves out on it."

They ate their sandwiches looking at a view of distant blue hills and country which looked like a patchwork—the green and yellow of the fields criss-crossed by the dark green and brown of the hedges. The corn was ripening and the wheatfields were yellow-gold and the oats a pale creamy yellow. When they had finished their lunch they lay on their backs in the sun and watched a lark soaring up until it was a tiny speck in the blue sky, its song was the only sound to be heard except for the ponies cropping grass.

Then Jonathan spotted a kestrel and they watched while it hovered patiently in one spot and then swooped down in a lightning dart.

"Some poor little mouse," Debbie said. She wondered if Snoozy was all right? And what about Appy and Tite, did Mrs. Austin get the sort of fish they liked, and was Tim getting enough green food for the rabbits and guinea-pigs? Hammish would miss her and Wiggs had to have bread-and-milk put out for him at night, which is when hedge-hogs wake up and come out.

"Wake up, Deb!" Jonathan said impatiently. "I've said at least three times that we could go on again now."

"Sorry." Debbie got up. "Let's gallop to the end of the down, if it's not too far for the ponies, and then look for bilberries."

They mounted, and before Jonathan was settled in his saddle Kit-Kat was snatching at his bit and prancing eagerly.

"Come on!" Jonathan shouted. "We'll have a super gallop." He let Kit-Kat go and the pony plunged forward going into a fast canter. At that moment a big sheep-dog bounded out of the bushes and jumped at Kit-Kat, barking excitedly.

Kit-Kat shied and nearly unseated Jonathan, who lost a stirrup and let the reins slip through his fingers. The pony went off at a gallop with the dog racing beside him, yelping and barking.

Jonathan shouted at him, "Get away. Shut up." The dog took no notice and it seemed to make Kit-Kat go even faster. He had some difficulty in finding his dangling stirrup iron at a headlong gallop, and when he was firmly in the saddle he shortened his reins to get Kit-Kat under control. He'd never gone so fast—rather super, he thought, with the wind whistling past his face and Kit-Kat's hoof-beats drumming on the turf.

It gave him an uneasy feeling when he realized his pony was out of control. He *couldn't* steady him or pull him up. No need to worry though, Jonathan thought, there was room to gallop for miles. They could go on until Kit-Kat had had enough and then ease up gently, better than pulling at him.

He looked ahead between Kit-Kat's pricked ears. *Was* there room to gallop for miles? He could see a ragged line of bushes and a post or two in front of them and beyond this the ground appeared to drop away steeply. A quarry? A pond? Jonathan suddenly felt alarmed. He'd got to avoid galloping into it.

He tried to pull up but Kit-Kat was galloping with his head stretched out and the reins might not have been there for all the use they were. Jonathan threw his weight back in the saddle and pulled against him, calling "Whoa", but Kit-Kat went galloping on, nearer and nearer to the quarry.

Turn him, Jonathan thought desperately. He

pulled on his right hand rein to get Kit-Kat's head round, using the correct Aid at the same time, but it wasn't easy at a gallop and it had no effect. With the reins at full length he'd no control.

Throw himself off? A nasty idea but not as bad as falling into a quarry, and if Kit-Kat were riderless he might stop and not get hurt. Jonathan glanced at the ground which seemed to be moving past very fast. He'd have to——

There was a thundering of hooves on his left as a grey horse came up beside him and a voice said "Pull to the right—hard."

Jonathan did so, no longer feeling frightened now that he had help. The grey horse was pushing Kit-Kat across to the right, the rider's leg bumping against Jonathan's and his shoe pressing against Jonathan's shin. He had hold of Kit-Kat's rein and was checking him so that Jonathan was able to pull him in and get his head round. They were turning—going slower too—and with a feeling of huge relief Jonathan saw that they were riding along beside the bushes above the quarry and not straight at them.

"Okay now. Whoa, pony!" They came to a halt and Jonathan leaned over Kit-Kat's neck while he got his breath. Then he sat up and looked at the rider of the grey. He was a boy of about sixteen, not much older than Mark.

"Thanks awfully," Jonathan said. "I was going to jump off."

"I'm glad you didn't. People generally get hurt if they bale out. Going down into a quarry'd be worse though."

Jonathan looked back. He could see the quarry clearly now. The railings guarding it had broken away and the little stunted bushes wouldn't have stopped Kit-Kat. He felt rather sick as he looked at the stones below. "Thanks awfully," he said again. "Your grey was simply marvellous."

"He's very steady and sensible. I can do practically anything with him."

Looking across the down, Jonathan saw Debbie and Puck coming at a careful, controlled but fast canter. "Here's Debbie, my sister. She got left behind when Kit-Kat got away with me."

They trotted back to meet her and told each other their names. The boy was Philip Renton and the grey was called Silver Flash.

"He's smashing," Debbie said, when they had met and were all riding along together.

"So's yours," Philip said, looking at Kit-Kat. "He's very fast. Is he a thoroughbred?"

"He's not pure bred, but he's got some thoroughbred blood," Jonathan explained. "He's never got away with me before though he's always keen. A dog dashed out scaring him just as we were starting to gallop. He shied and darn nearly had me off, by the time I'd got myself straight again he was going flat out. He stuck his nose out quite straight and the reins just didn't work."

"Try a martingale or one of those special nosebands," Philip suggested. "I should get expert advice."

"It might be a good idea," Jonathan agreed.

"We haven't found any bilberries," exclaimed Debbie.

"There aren't any on the short grass," Philip said. "There might be some over there." He pointed to a large patch of what looked like heather and long, rough grass.

They rode across and dismounted. While they looked for, and found, a few of the little bluish round berries Jonathan and Debbie told Philip about the caravan.

"It must be terrific fun," he said. "Are you tied to a tight schedule or could you come and camp near us?"

They rode on and he told them where he lived. His father farmed and Philip was sure he would let them camp there. "We're getting up a Hare and Hounds chase on ponies next Friday. If you could come then and ride in it that'd be fun."

"Oh yes!" Debbie exclaimed. "I'd love that."

Philip told them how to find the farm and gave them the address written on an old envelope. "Come the night before," he said. "It starts at two and Mum's giving everyone tea afterwards. There'll be about a dozen hounds and two hares. We're using shavings for laying the trail, not as messy as paper and light to carry."

"Thank you very much, we'd love to come," Debbie said.

"Will you hold your pony all right?" Philip asked Jonathan. "The course is twisty with lots of little jumps. Dad planned it like that so people don't get galloping and out of control. And there are two jumps side by side, small and medium. We go in a circle so the small kids can keep on the inside and not be left behind."

"It sounds marvellous," Debbie said, thinking with relief that if Puck couldn't jump the larger jumps she could go over the smaller ones.

"I'll hold Kit-Kat all right," Jonathan said confidently. "It was because the dog startled him that he went off and if he hadn't shied and nearly had me off I could've stopped him then."

"It wouldn't have mattered if the quarry hadn't been there," said Philip.

Debbie shuddered, she had been too far behind to see clearly what had happened but it sounded horrid. "Is it time to meet the others?" she asked.

Jonathan looked at his watch. "Half an hour. Do you know how long it'll take us to get to where the down joins the road at Stoneyford?"

"About twenty minutes," Philip answered and Jonathan looked pleased. They were going to be punctual which was satisfactory, and he couldn't help thinking how easily they might not have arrived safely. He tried to thank Philip again but he wouldn't let him.

Stoneyford was a tiny hamlet with a stream where they watered the ponies. Then the caravan came up and Ajax drank too while Jonathan introduced Philip to his mother and Lucy and Mark. He told them how Philip had come to his rescue.

Mrs. Manning thanked Philip and admired Silver Flash. Then she asked him to have tea with them but he said regretfully that he had some way to go home and mustn't stay.

"See you for the Hare and Hounds," he said, and repeated the date and his address before riding away.

"A nice boy," Mrs. Manning said. "Now we must find somewhere to camp tonight."

"Your mouth's blue," Lucy told Debbie. "Is it from eating bilberries?"

"We only found a few," Debbie replied. "The down was super except for the quarry."

"We must be thankful there wasn't an accident," her mother said. "Now let's forget it. Except that I think it'd be a good idea to get some advice about another bit for Kit-Kat, Jonathan."

"I'll ask the Pony Club people," Jonathan agreed.

"There's a farm over there," Mark pointed. "Should we try it?"

After a little persuasion the farmer consented and showed them a nice site in the corner of a big orchard. The horses were turned out in a field and then the work of making camp began. It went much more quickly than it had the first evening and they sat down to supper punctually.

"An early night won't hurt any of us," Mrs. Manning said, "and there'll be plenty of time for everyone to wash really properly."

"Hardly worth it seeing how quickly we get dirty again," Jonathan remarked.

But his mother put both big kettles on the fire for a supply of hot water and said everyone was to go to bed clean.

CHAPTER FOUR

MIDGET'S PORTRAIT

EVERYONE slept well, they were used to the beds which had seemed rather strange on the first night. Debbie was the first to wake and she sat up and pulled back the curtain over the little window above her bunk and looked out. It was a dull morning with a heavy grey sky but, as Mrs. Manning said at breakfast, they were bound to have some days which were wet, or windy and cold.

By mid-morning it was raining. They ate lunch inside the caravan, crowded round the little table. Wet raincoats were a nuisance, but the oil-stove was useful for making cocoa. A hot drink kept you going, Mrs. Manning said, especially on a wet day. The rain stopped in the afternoon and they began to look out for somewhere to camp. The first farm they asked at refused them and Mrs. Manning began to look worried.

They came to a small village. Mark and Debbie were riding ahead and Lucy was giving Locket a little walk. Suddenly a little dog came out of a big gateway and Locket bustled up to it.

"Another Yorkie!" cried Lucy, and a middle-aged lady coming out of the gateway exclaimed, "A Yorkshire terrier like Midget!"

The two dogs were sniffing at each other, when Locket gave a little bounce, inviting a game,

Midget jumped round excitedly. Then she turned and ran back inside the gateway and stopped, looking back with a little bark and Locket ran after her. They began to play and raced off together.

"Locket," Lucy called, but Locket took no notice.

The lady laughed. "They've made friends very quickly."

The caravan had stopped and Debbie and Mark had turned back to see what was happening.

"May I go and get her?" asked Lucy. She could see the two dogs playing on a lawn in front of a large house.

"Of course," said the woman. She was patting Puck. "I do like your ponies. Are you on a camping-riding holiday?"

"Yes," replied Mrs. Manning. "We've just started. We live near Chelsdon."

"It must be great fun. Are you in a hurry? Can't you stay to tea? Or are you too superior to have a meal indoors in an ordinary house?"

"Not in the least," Mrs. Manning laughed. "It's very kind of you but we must find somewhere to camp. We had difficulty one night and we've asked at one farm near here and were refused. It's rather a worry and we mustn't be too late finding somewhere."

"Stay here," said the woman. "We've got a field. We'd love to have you and your ponies, and the Yorkie, Midget—she's my daughter's—will love having her."

"Thank you very much, that'd be marvellous," Mrs. Manning said gratefully.

"I'll show you the way in. My name's Thursby. My husband's somewhere about, I know he'll be delighted for you to stay."

She led the way to a back gate and Mrs. Manning and Lucy managed the sharp turn in successfully. Then they pulled up in a big yard.

"You can stay here if you like," Mrs. Thursby said. "There's the field," she pointed to a gate. "There's plenty of keep in it and a water trough. There's a tap here which is drinking water, quite handy for you."

"You are kind," Mrs. Manning said. "I think we'd be better in the yard than in the field as the grass is so wet now."

Mrs. Thursby opened a door. "This used to be the tack-room. You could use it to hang wet coats in."

Debbie saw a long row of dusty rosettes and prize-cards. "Who won those?" she asked.

"My children, Helen and Gerald, they're grown-up now and it's very dull without any ponies. What are yours called?"

They told her the ponies' names and their own and then Lucy said anxiously, "I must find Locket."

"Come along," Mrs. Thursby said. "I'll show you round. Do come too," she invited Mrs. Manning. "Can the children manage?"

"Oh indeed yes. They're quite capable of looking after everything," Mrs. Manning answered. Now they'd found somewhere to camp she felt quite different.

"Then come and see what those two Yorkies are

up to and then we'll have tea. Lucy could come back and fetch the others."

She led them through a little gate and along a path round the house to the front where Locket and Midget were playing on the lawn.

"What a pretty house!" exclaimed Mrs. Manning. It was built of grey stone, the windows had little diamond-shaped panes which twinkled as the sun began to shine through the clouds; a coat of arms was carved over the front door and the chimneys had curious patterns on them.

"It's an old manor-house and it's never been altered or spoilt," Mrs. Thursby explained.

"It really is beautiful," said Mrs. Manning. "I'd adore to sketch it. I brought my paints just in case we stopped somewhere very nice."

"Do stay and paint it," Mrs. Thursby said.

"I'd like to, if it's fine tomorrow," said Mrs. Manning. She painted very well and sometimes sold pictures. "But the children will want to go on somewhere new, I expect, and it's their holiday."

"Let's talk about it at tea," Mrs. Thursby said. She took them indoors, with Locket and Midget who had to be persuaded to break off their game, and into a big old-fashioned kitchen where she began to prepare tea. After they had washed—"most necessary," Mrs. Manning remarked, "as caravanning makes you so grubby"—Lucy went out of the back door to fetch the others.

They had turned out Ajax and the ponies and hung up the tack (Ajax's collar and driving pad were very heavy) in the tack-room and they left Tiger there with his own bed which they had brought.

Colonel Thursby was as nice as Mrs. Thursby and during tea he told the boys about pig-sticking and hunting tigers on elephants in India. He had a golden spaniel called Brandy.

The sun came out and Mrs. Thursby looked out of the window and said it would be fine tomorrow. "So you'll be able to do a painting of the house."

"Would you mind staying here a day?" Mrs. Manning asked the children. "I expect a day off would be good for Ajax."

"We wouldn't mind. We can ride and explore," said Mark.

"Do you like swimming?" asked Colonel Thursby.

"Rather!" Jonathan said enthusiastically.

"Friends of ours here have a pool in their garden which they let us and our visitors use. I'll take you along there."

"Thank you awfully, sir," Mark said. "We'd love that."

"What about the girls?" Colonel Thursby asked.

"I don't much want to, thank you," Debbie answered, because Lucy wasn't allowed to swim, "and I've no swim-suit," she added thankfully, for Lucy was apt to see through Debbie and insist that she didn't mind being left out.

"You boys got any kit?" asked the colonel.

Jonathan had, he never went away without his, if there was a stream of any sort Jonathan would be in it. Mark hadn't but Mrs. Thursby said she could fix him up with an old one of her children's and she took him off to choose one and then

Colonel Thursby took them to the pool for a quick dip.

Lucy and Debbie helped Mrs. Manning get supper and make the beds. They cooked on the oil-stove because the yard wasn't a suitable place to to make a fire.

Supper was ready when the boys returned, with sleek wet hair and a shining clean look. Colonel Thursby asked if they had everything they needed and Mrs. Manning said they had. "But we can't erect the tent in the yard, pegs wouldn't go into the ground, so might the boys sleep in the tack-room?"

"Of course. Good idea, they'll be in the dry. Very hard floor though."

"We've got air-beds, sir," Mark said.

"Luxurious fellows," Colonel Thursby remarked. "I slept on the ground when I started soldiering."

"I don't mind how many days we stay here if we can swim all the time," Jonathan said at supper, and Mark agreed.

The next morning Mrs. Manning settled herself in the garden and began her picture of the house. The boys went to the pool and Debbie and Lucy cooked a very special lunch. They went to the butcher in the village and bought beef-steak and kidney for a pie which they made in a little oven fitted over the oil-stove. It was a great success.

In the afternoon Debbie and Jonathan went for a ride while Mark and Lucy cleaned Ajax's harness. It took them a long time as there was so much of it but it looked very nice when the brass was polished.

Jonathan and Debbie rode round the lanes exploring and they came back by a bridle-path where they could canter. Puck went very well (he always did) being keen but not a puller. It was sickening for Lucy not being able to ride for a whole year, Debbie thought, they'd had such fun riding together before her illness.

In the evening Mrs. Manning showed them her picture which was just like the manor and very pretty. "I'll finish it tomorrow," she said.

"It's charming," remarked Mrs. Thursby, who had come to see if there was anything they needed. She asked if Mrs. Manning sold her pictures and if she might buy it.

"I sell them whenever I can, but I'd like to give you this. It's been so kind of you to have us all here."

"Thank you very much, it's a lovely present," Mrs. Thursby said.

"Animals are what Mummie's best at," Debbie told her.

"She did a super one of Locket for me for Christmas," Lucy said, "it's exactly like her."

"Would you paint Midget?" Mrs. Thursby asked eagerly. "I want a present for Helen's birthday and she'd love that. Could you possibly stay a little longer, and of course I must buy this one."

"Could we stay?" Mrs. Manning asked the children. "Dogs take longer than houses as they don't keep still! Of course I could come over from home to paint Midget."

"Helen lives up north and she's coming to fetch Midget on their way home next week," Mrs.

Thursby explained, "I've been looking after her while they're abroad."

"I don't mind how long we stay," Jonathan said, "the swimming pool's a very good one."

"And this is as nice as anywhere to camp," Debbie said.

Mark and Lucy agreed with her, so Mrs. Manning said she'd start Midget's portrait the next day as soon as she had finished the one of the house.

"What about Philip and the Hare and Hounds?" Debbie asked. "It's on Friday."

"Oh dear, I'd forgotten about that," her mother said. "I shan't have finished painting Midget by then."

Mark and Jonathan looked at each other, both with the same idea. Mark spoke, "Couldn't we go by ourselves?"

"Why not?" asked Mrs. Thursby. "I'm sure they could manage perfectly well."

"Oh do let us," Debbie urged. "It'd be super fun. Only where would Mummie sleep?" she added thoughtfully.

"We'd all sleep in the caravan and she could have the tent," Jonathan suggested.

"Certainly not," Mrs. Thursby protested. "She'll stay with us, we'll love having her and she'll have more time for painting. I want her to do one of Brandy too as a present for my husband."

"I haven't said they can go off alone," Mrs. Manning said laughing. "I must think about it. I suppose it's all right for you to go to the Rentons? You've only Philip's invitation, his parents may not want campers."

"I know the Rentons slightly, well enough to ring them up and ask about it," said Mrs. Thursby. "And I could ask them to keep an eye on the children, just enough to help if needed but not to take charge." She smiled at them and Debbie thought how kind she was. "And I'm sure they're very nice people."

"I'll have to ask Lucy's mother what she thinks about it," Mrs. Manning said. "I know Mark's won't mind."

After some telephoning it was arranged that the children were to go to the Rentons on Thursday and come back on Saturday. They were to ring up on Thursday evening to tell Mrs. Manning that they had arrived.

"We can keep in touch by 'phone and we could run over there in the car if you were anxious," Mrs. Thursby told Mrs. Manning, "it's only about ten miles."

"I'm sure they'll be all right," Mrs. Manning said. "Nothing's likely to happen in two days, surely."

But it wasn't two days, and a great deal was going to happen.

CHAPTER FIVE

HARE AND HOUNDS

"THIS is the place." Mark nodded towards a white gate leading to a large grey house. There was a paddock in front of it where several horses were grazing, and behind it a range of farm buildings.

"It looks jolly decent," Debbie said. "I hope they're nice." Now they had reached the Rentons she was wishing they hadn't come; it was difficult to say, Here we are, to people they didn't know.

"Mrs. Thursby said they were," remarked Lucy, who wasn't troubled by shyness.

"Here's Philip," exclaimed Jonathan, and Debbie felt relieved as she saw him coming down the drive leading Silver Flash. He waved when he saw them. After he had turned out Silver Flash in the paddock he came to them.

"Glad you've got here. We've got you somewhere to camp near the house."

He took them past the front entrance and round to the farmyard. They went through this into a little paddock.

"Dad thought this would be a good place, and Mum says come to the house for anything you want. The ponies can go in the next field."

He helped them unharness Ajax and showed them a shed where they could keep their tack.

They had just turned out the horses when Mr. Renton came to find them, and any shyness they may have felt was driven away at once by his friendly manner. He made them laugh when he told them how he'd once gone camping and got a cow in the tent in the night.

"No cows here," he said, "as long as you shut the gates, and anyone who doesn't shut gates oughtn't to be let loose in the country but kept on a lead with their dog! I like your Boxer," he patted Tiger. "He doesn't fight? We've a couple of sheep-dogs."

"Oh no, he's very good-tempered, sir," Jonathan assured him. "But he growls if anyone comes near the camp."

"Just what you want," Mr. Renton said. "Philip, show them where to get water—there's a tap near by. And here's my wife, she'll have you all indoors in proper beds if you don't look out!"

He went off to the farm and Mrs. Renton came across the paddock. She was quite unlike a farmer's wife, being small and frail. She was quite different from Mr. Renton but just as nice.

"I'm so glad you've come," she said, "Mrs. Thursby told me you're quite self-supporting and able to look after yourselves but be sure and come and ask for anything you want."

They thanked her and said they would.

"And I've enough beds, all ready and aired, if you'd like to sleep indoors? I'm sure that would be more comfortable."

The children tried not to laugh—it was just what Mr. Renton had said.

"Dad told them you'd try and get them indoors," Philip said grinning. "If I'd a tent I'd sleep out here."

"As long as it doesn't *rain*," Mrs. Renton said rather anxiously. "Now have you plenty to eat?"

"Heaps, thank you," Lucy replied. "We bought chops. I'm chief cook and I'm going to fry them for supper."

"You must come to us for a meal," Mrs. Renton said. "And what about hot baths?"

"Mummie's always heating water for us to wash," said Jonathan.

"Come to supper tomorrow," Mrs. Renton invited them, "you'll be tired after riding all afternoon so you won't want to cook a meal, then you can have baths first."

"That's awfully kind," Lucy said. "Thank you."

Mrs. Renton admired Locket and then, after reminding them to come and ask for anything they needed, she left.

"Can I help at all?" Philip asked.

"Sure, getting the tent up," Mark answered.

"Is it okay to make a fire?" Debbie asked.

"Yes, only keep it small," Philip replied. He showed them a great stack of firewood and they all carried some back to the camp. Jonathan started the fire while Mark and Philip erected the tent.

"Stay to supper with us, Philip? Lucy asked, brandishing a frying-pan.

"I'd like to, if you've enough?"

"Heaps," Debbie said. "We bought masses of chops and there's stacks of tinned stuff."

It really was rather fun to be on their own, not

that Mrs. Manning wasn't awfully nice and the most perfect person to go caravanning with, but as they sat round the fire eating the chops, and fried chips and tomatoes, they had a lovely feeling of independence.

"I say!" Mark exclaimed. "We never rang up. We simply mustn't forget or Aunt Di will think something's gone wrong. May I 'phone, Philip?"

Philip took him to the house, and when he returned he said Mrs. Renton had told him they must come indoors if it rained. "But it won't." He looked up at the clear sky.

"It'll be dark soon, we'd better start going to bed," Debbie said.

It took longer than they expected (they washed with special thoroughness in case Mrs. Renton had thought they were dirty), and it was dark before they were all in bed. When they had settled down Debbie remembered they hadn't put out the fire, so she called to Mark, who got up and put water on it. The sizzle of the ashes had only just died away when Tiger growled and Locket yapped.

It was Philip. His mother had sent him to make sure they were all right. "I'll report you're all okay and asleep," he said. "G'night."

"She's terribly kind but terribly fussy," Lucy said as they settled down again.

"Thank goodness it's fine," Debbie said next morning. "I hate having to ride in a mack."

They had finished breakfast and tidied up, luckily just before Mrs. Renton visited them (and she seemed impressed). Now they were preparing for the afternoon. While Jonathan and Debbie groomed their ponies Lucy and Mark cleaned the tack.

"When we've done the ponies let's groom Ajax," Debbie suggested, rubbing her body-brush on the curry-comb to remove the dust.

"I'm going to plait Kit-Kat's mane," Jonathan said. "Have you any black cotton and needles, or rubber bands?"

"No. Mummie's got the sewing things," Debbie replied.

"You could ask Mrs. Renton," Lucy suggested. "I think she'd like us to ask for things, she keeps coming to see if we want anything."

Jonathan went to the house and returned with a handful of rubber bands. While he plaited up Kit-Kat Debbie and Mark groomed Ajax. This took a long time as there was such a lot of him, and even Mark couldn't reach his forelock to brush it, but he obligingly lowered his head. When they'd finished he looked very nice.

Lunch was a scramble because Lucy forgot to start cooking in time, so they ate bread and cheese and bananas while they changed into clean shirts (and Debbie and Jonathan into jodhpurs instead of jeans).

It was just two o'clock when they rode round to the front of the house. The ponies looked smart with well-cleaned tack, and Philip had given them some hoof-oil, Kit-Kat's mane was, Lucy said, a good finishing touch.

They found about a dozen children on ponies and some unmounted. Lucy and Mark joined these, and they were told that Philip and a girl called Sandra were the Hares.

"What have they got in their haversacks?" Lucy asked.

"Shavings for the trail," Mrs. Renton told her. "They aren't as untidy as paper and they soon rot away. Philip rode round this morning and left some more haversacks along the route for them to pick up."

The Hares set off and Mr. Renton stood looking at his watch. The Hares were to have a start. Debbie felt excited and a tiny bit nervous. Puck always behaved perfectly but she'd never ridden in anything like this and didn't know what to expect. Jonathan was feeling anxious too, it would be awful if Kit-Kat played up or ran away again. He'd said he was sure he could hold him but—

"Right," Mr. Renton called. "Off you go. Follow the trail and only small people may cut corners."

Jonathan took Kit-Kat to the front because he fretted if he was kept back. Debbie was content to follow with the half-dozen who had ponies about the same size as Puck. Four or five small children trotted along behind with a grown-up riding a slow, fat cob.

The trail was easy to see, wisps of white shavings right across the first field, and they cantered at a smart pace. A boy on a black pony and a girl on a skewbald led and Jonathan kept close behind them. Kit-Kat was going smoothly and Jonathan knew that as long as he wasn't pulled at he wouldn't hot up.

They reached the first jump, which was made out of the fence, neatly trimmed and much lower at one end. "For the babies," said the girl as they came up to it. It was wide and they jumped it abreast. Smashing fun, thought Jonathan, steadying Kit-Kat on landing, like a point-to-point.

They had jumped into a big meadow but they weren't to gallop across it, for the trail turned and took them over another jump into the next field, twisted again and they jumped some sheep hurdles into a field where the trail split into two.

"Which one?" asked the girl on the skewbald whose name was Caroline.

"One's a false trail," said Michael, the boy riding the black pony.

The others came up and everyone talked at once. Debbie joined Jonathan and asked how Kit-Kat was going.

"Okay. It's terrific fun," Jonathan said.

Michael was all for going straight on. "The other trail, going to the left, takes us back toward the house and we shan't be going back yet," he urged.

Caroline was sure that the left one was the true trail. "It looks wrong so it's sure to be right, they're being cunning."

"Can't some of us go one way and the rest go the other?" Debbie suggested, but Michael said they must keep together and they all went straight on. They crossed one field and went through a gate, which they carefully shut, into another field where the trail vanished.

"Blast! This is the false one. Back!" Michael said, turning his pony.

They dashed back, grumbling at the gate, and met the smaller children who turned round and raced along, keeping up for a while.

Coming to where the trail forked they took the other one without losing any time. "Got to make up lost time," said Michael, sending his black along at a good pace.

"We *must* catch them," Caroline said.

Jonathan let Kit-Kat go ahead and Caroline's skewbald came up beside him. The trail led to a wood and they pulled up at some slip-rails. Michael jumped off and threw his reins to Caroline.

"Hang on to Cinders," he said and began to take down the top rail. He pulled out one end of the next rail leaving it sloping down to the ground where the smallest ponies could step over it. He swung himself onto Cinders and followed Jonathan over the rails. "Last one through puts the rails back," he shouted over his shoulder.

A ride—a wide path—led straight across the wood and they pounded down it, dodging whippy branches, and came to more slip-rails. Michael was off his pony before he'd pulled up and had the top rails down, and they were out of the wood and in a large field.

Michael and Caroline went off at a cracking pace, the trail was clearly seen on the grass. Jonathan kept close behind them with Kit-Kat going well. All at once there was a blurred flash of white and chestnut and someone falling—the skewbald had slipped up throwing Caroline in front of Kit-Kat.

To Jonathan's horror he saw her right under his pony who seemed to swerve in the air. He pulled up and Kit-Kat stopped dead. Jonathan jumped off and turned to look. Caroline was on her feet and the skewbald was getting up.

"Are you okay?" he asked, hardly able to believe she wasn't hurt.

"Yes. Is Paint-box all right?" She caught the skewbald and looked at him. "He seems okay."

Michael had stopped and turned back. "What happened? Are you all right, Caroline?"

"Absolutely. Paint-box slipped up. I was right under Jonathan's pony and he sort of hopped over me, he was marvellous."

Jonathan patted Kit-Kat. "He's very clever and sure-footed, that's how he got his name."

"Come on then," Michael said impatiently, and they all rode on across the field. But now Jonathan was feeling relaxed and happy. Kit-Kat wasn't a tear-away that he couldn't hold, he'd been marvellous avoiding Caroline and he'd stopped at once. It showed he'd only bolted because the dog had scared him.

The trail took them into a grassy lane, and here Mr. Renton had prepared some unexpected jumps. The first was a row of wooden hen-coops, not big but unusual, and Michael's pony Cinders stopped dead, snorting with surprise. Paint-box and Kit-Kat refused too.

Debbie rode forward, confident on Puck. "I'll give you a lead," and she popped Puck over. The next jump was a low double made of bales of straw. At the end of the lane there was a red and white Road Closed and Puck jumped this too without any fuss. So Debbie was leading when they came into the last field and it was she who saw the Hares first. "There they are!"

Philip looked back and then set his grey horse going with his partner hustling her pony along too. Debbie pushed Puck into a gallop but Kit-Kat passed them with Cinders close behind. The Hares had reached the end of the field where Mr. Renton and the spectators were waiting and it became a race between Kit-Kat and Cinders as to who would finish first. Kit-Kat drew ahead to win and Debbie was racing Caroline, but Paint-box was too fast for Puck.

They all pulled up and stood in groups, talking and laughing while stragglers came in and Mr. Renton checked that everyone was present.

"Kit-Kat was wonderful," Caroline said.

"He's awfully fast," said Michael admiringly.

"He's got some thoroughbred blood in him," Jonathan explained with pride. "It was a smashing ride," he told Mr. Renton, "and super jumps."

"Splendid!" Mr. Renton said, "Philip's organized horse-lines for you to tie up your ponies while we have tea, so come along everyone."

After an enormous and delicious tea everyone went home. It was rather nice not to have to cook supper and hot baths were very pleasant.

"It was lucky meeting Philip and getting invited," Lucy said as they went back to the caravan at bed-time.

"They're awfully nice," Debbie agreed. "And it's not very far from home so we may see Philip again."

"All because of Kit-Kat," said Jonathan.

CHAPTER SIX

JONATHAN WAKES UP

THEY were late starting next morning. They had meant to get away in good time but they all slept rather late, and then packing up took longer than they had expected. When they were ready to leave Mrs. Renton said she'd like to take a photo of them and there was a delay while she fetched her camera. They all posed in front of the caravan, but first Tiger and then Kit-Kat spoilt a snap by moving. So it was twelve o'clock before they left, with promises to meet again to Philip, and many thank-you's to Mr. and Mrs. Renton.

"It doesn't matter being late," Mark said as they turned into the road. "It's not far and we'll be back in time for supper."

Silver Flash and the other horses in the paddock in front of the house came up to the fence and whinnied as the ponies went past.

"Saying good-bye to us," Debbie said. "We had a fine time and the Rentons are awfully nice."

They made a brief stop for lunch (slices of tinned meat with salad and then fruit). Jonathan looked at the map and said it was only seven miles and they'd be back in plenty of time to get camped in daylight. It would be fun, Debbie thought, to tell her mother about the Hare and Hounds.

Mark was riding Kit-Kat and Jonathan was on Puck. Lucy was driving and Debbie was sitting beside her when she noticed something odd about the way Ajax was walking.

"Stop, Lucy. Something's wrong with Ajax, I hope he's not lame. I believe he's lost a shoe."

Lucy drew up at the side of the road and they both got down quickly. "I was just noticing that he sounded different somehow," she said.

A quick inspection showed that he had cast his off fore shoe. The boys came back to see why they had stopped.

"Well!" said Mark. "We're late already and goodness knows where the nearest blacksmith is. I hope there's one near. We can't take Ajax along the road very far."

They looked at each other in dismay. "How will we get him to the smith then?" asked Debbie.

"We'll have to leave the caravan here so we can lead him on the grass at the road-side," Mark said. "Or it'd knock his hoof about and make him lame, but perhaps there's a blacksmith near here."

"There's a village just ahead," Jonathan said. "Shall we go on and ask about a blacksmith?"

"Good idea," Mark said. "Bring him along slowly."

The boys rode on and Lucy and Debbie walked beside Ajax. "Bring him slowly—as if he ever went anything but slowly," Lucy said. "Poor old boy!" she patted his glossy neck. "He's always so good and no trouble, this is bad luck."

Quite soon they saw the boys trotting back towards them. "Terrific luck!" Jonathan said as they pulled up. "A blacksmith in the village and it's quite close."

"Good," said Lucy, "but it'll make us most terribly late. We'd better ring up and tell Mrs. Thursby."

"We can do that while Ajax is being shod," said Mark. "There's a hill in this village, the steepest we've met, and the forge is at the bottom. We'll need to put the brakes on hard. Will you hang on to the brake handle, Lucy?"

"Not the wheel skids?" asked Jonathan.

"I don't think it's as steep as all that," Mark said. "After all, we came up it on the way here and it wasn't so bad. But if Ajax has any difficulty in holding back the caravan we'll stop and put them under the wheels."

"How do they work?" Lucy asked.

"They go under the back wheels so they can't turn, they strap on to the wheels," Mark explained. He led Ajax and Lucy sat in the driving seat to work the brakes. Debbie and Jonathan came behind with the ponies.

The village was on a long hill with cottages on each side of the road and half-way down there was a little old grey church. The caravan went down slowly with Lucy holding the brake handle hard on and Ajax leaning back against the breeching (which was fastened to the shafts each side so that he could hold back the caravan going downhill). The brakes made a grating noise but they held perfectly.

At the bottom of the hill Mark said "Okay, Lucy. Brakes off. The blacksmith lives up this lane."

They turned up a side turning and stopped outside the forge. But instead of the clanging on an anvil and the bellows blowing a fire—everything they had expected—there was silence and the door was closed.

"It's shut!" Jonathan exclaimed.

"What a nuisance!" said Mark. "The chap who told us where it was never said he was closed. Of course, Saturday afternoon, we might have guessed."

"What shall we do now?" Debbie asked.

"We can't go on," Jonathan pointed out.

"Perhaps we could find the blacksmith and get him to shoe Ajax, if we told him we must go on," Lucy suggested.

Mark looked round and pointed to a cottage near the forge. "He probably lives there. I'll go and ask."

Before he could do this a woman came out of the cottage and approached them. "Are you looking for Mr. Appleton, the smith? He's gone to the town and won't be back till late tonight. It's his half-day, Saturday, and he knocks off at twelve."

"Oh help!" Jonathan said. "We've had it!"

"What is it you want done?" asked the woman, looking at them with interest. She had very red cheeks and brown eyes and a most friendly smile. "I'm sorry my husband's not here," she added, so they knew she was Mrs. Appleton.

Mark explained briefly. "We can't go on. It seems the only thing we can do is camp here till Monday. Is there a field anywhere near we could use?"

"I dessay we can find somewhere," Mrs. Appleton said cheerfully. "We've a little field that goes with the forge and I reckon it'd do for your animals but its all on the hill, no use for your van. Could you put it in the orchard yonder?" She pointed and the children saw a small grassy plot with a few gnarled old apple trees at the side of the cottage. "T'is flat and there's water at the tap here."

"That'd do marvellously," Mark said. "Thank you."

"You're welcome," Mrs. Appleton replied.

"And it's handy for Ajax, he needn't go along a road until he's been shod," Debbie said.

It was a little difficult to get the caravan into the orchard as there was a sharp turn and the gate wasn't very wide, but Lucy was an expert driver now and she managed it with Mark watching to see the wheels wouldn't touch and calling out to her. Ajax was very steady and never rushed. They parked the caravan in a corner and took Ajax out of the shafts.

Mrs. Appleton showed the way to the field, which was half-way up the hill. There was a path from the forge which went behind the cottages at the lower end of the village street and came out half-way up where there was a gate into the field. The gate was just back from the road and the path came out in the street. There was a water trough and enough keep for a few days. Ajax had a good ration of oats and chaff and the ponies had a small feed every evening. They had made a point of keeping the corn locker full by buying fodder regularly, and Mr. Renton had filled it up for them and refused any payment.

"Shall Lucy and I telephone now?" Debbie suggested. So the boys went back to start making a camp, and the girls went along the street to the post office which was also the village stores.

"This place is called Kensleigh," Debbie remarked, looking at the sign above the door. "Lucky I saw that, as we'll have to tell Mummie where it is that we've got stuck. I hope she won't be fussed."

"So do I," Lucy said, "because it's going to be fun. Two more nights really on our own, not even Mrs. Renton asking if we're all right."

Mrs. Thursby answered the telephone and called Mrs. Manning. While her mother was coming Debbie explained what had happened.

"Bad luck!" Mrs. Thursby said. "But never mind, you've got your house with you and can stop anywhere! Have you found somewhere to camp?"

Debbie said they had, and then her mother came and she had to explain everything all over again. "But we're absolutely okay, Mummie, honestly," she ended. "A field for the horses, and the caravan's in an orchard near the blacksmith's cottage. Mrs. Appleton, his wife, is awfully decent."

"That sounds all right." Her mother didn't seem to be anxious, Debbie thought with relief. "Are you short of money?"

"Oh no." They had started with enough to buy food and oats and chaff, but thanks to the Rentons' hospitality they hadn't spent much. "We've heaps."

"Ring up tomorrow morning, just to let me know how you all are."

Debbie said they would and rang off.

"Money," said Lucy as they walked back. She'd had Locket under her arm, and now she put her down and let her run along the path back to the camp. "We'll have to pay for Ajax's shoe and shoeing's awfully dear."

"Oh golly! I forgot that," Debbie said. "Mummie asked if we were short and I said we'd heaps. And Ajax may need more than one shoe. Horses are generally shod all round and that means they all wear out at once."

"We needn't buy any food, there's masses of tins," Lucy said. "Even tinned meat for Tiger and Locket, and they love it. Milk is all we'll need to buy, and bread on Monday."

It wasn't worth making a fire just to heat some tinned food so they used the oil-stove. Lucy invented a dish she called Caravanner's Stew which she made by mixing tins of stewed beef, peas and soup and heating it all in one big pan. They ate it with spoons out of bowls and it was very good.

"I call that one of the major discoveries of the modern age, Lucy!" Mark said, passing his bowl for a second helping.

After supper Mr. Appleton returned and he came to see them. He was big and burly, just what a blacksmith ought to look like, Lucy said afterwards, and he was very pleasant. It was quite all right for them to use the field and orchard and he'd shoe Ajax first thing Monday. He looked at his feet and said he'd need another new one in front but the hind ones, though thin, would last a little longer he thought. He'd tell better when he had him in the forge and could see properly (it was getting dark). Then he asked if they were comfortable and had all they needed. After this he said goodnight and went back to his cottage where the light from a window made a square of yellow in the dusk.

They heard the cottage door shut. A little breeze ruffled their hair and an owl hooted quite close to them, then there was complete silence. Last night the Rentons had been at hand, now they were really on their own.

Jonathan woke and was wide awake in an instant. He sat up and Tiger, sleeping in his dog-bed between the boys, got up and moved to the doorway of the tent. The flap was up and Jonathan could see him silhouetted against the sky, his ears were pricked and he was alert and listening. What had woken them both?

Clip-clop. Horses on a road. The ponies had got out. Jonathan scrambled up and shook Mark's shoulder.

"Wake up. The ponies are out on the road."

Mark woke at once. "On the road?"

"Yes. Can't you hear them?"

Mark listened. "Yes! We must get them back before they go far, or a car comes along."

They pulled their jerseys and trousers on over their pyjamas and struggled into wellingtons.

"We must take the halters," Mark said. "We'd better leave Tiger in case he starts barking and wakes people."

Jonathan hitched his chain to the tent-pole and told him to "Stay" while Mark grabbed the halters.

Then they ran across the orchard and climbed over the gate.

"Which way?" Jonathan asked. "Up to the field or to the bottom of the hill?"

"To the bottom. They were definitely going down the hill," Mark replied. "Come to think of it it sounded like only one pony, not two."

"Then it's Kit-Kat," Jonathan said. "Puck never gets out by himself though he may follow. He must've stayed with Ajax. That's lucky."

They were running along the little side road which led from the forge into the village street. It was made dark by the cottages on each side but when they reached the road through the village it was quite light for the moon was shining, the houses in the moonlight looked almost white and those in shadow a dark grey with their windows like black squares.

"Lucky it's so light as the torch battery's pretty well done for," Mark observed. "Now which way, Jon? Not a sign of a pony."

"Not a sausage!" Jonathan said glumly. "He must've batted through the village and gone on along the road."

"I don't think he'll have gone far as we've not heard him racketting along the road, probably he's grazing at the road-side," Mark said. "Come on."

They ran along the road leading out of the village. It went perfectly straight for quite a long way, it was clearly lit by the moon and there was nothing in sight—no pony.

"He can't have gone so far as to be out of sight

unless he galloped," Mark said, dropping back to a walk. "We'd have heard him, you know what a row horse's hooves make on a road."

"Could he have got into a field through an open gate or a gap in a hedge?" Jonathan suggested.

They walked on, one on each side of the road, looking for anywhere a pony could have gone.

"Nowhere he could've got off the road and no side turnings he could have dashed up," said Mark presently. "We'd better go back."

They walked back looking in every field they passed. When they reached the village again Mark said "Let's go to the field and see which pony's missing."

They went up the silent village street and turned in at the opening half-way up the hill. There was the field gate—shut, but ponies usually get out through weak places in fences so that meant nothing.

Mark leaned on the gate and looked across the field which sloped downhill. The shadows under the trees were very dark. They heard the sound of a horse cropping grass and looked round. There was Ajax, grazing steadily. Did he eat all night, Jonathan wondered? Then he touched Mark's arm. "Two ponies. Look."

Under the nearest tree were two dark shapes, hearing Jonathan's voice they came up to the gate and nuzzled the boys' hands.

"Not our ponies," Mark said thankfully. "Come on, Jon, no need to lose any more sleep."

"It's one o'clock," Jonathan announced. "I can see by my watch. Some moon! Funny how that pony vanished. If we'd found him we'd not have known where to put him."

"There's something odd about it," Mark said slowly. "We both heard it distinctly and it stopped suddenly so it must be quite near or we'd have heard it getting fainter. I say—what's that?"

They were on the path down to the forge, just out of sight of the village street because the path went behind the houses to cut off the corner. A strange swishing sound came from the road and seemed to go down the hill before dying away as silently as it had begun.

"Blimey, another unexplained noise!" Jonathan exclaimed. "What a night!"

"I wish we could have seen whatever it was," Mark said, continuing down the path. "All very odd."

They were soon in bed again, but before falling asleep Jonathan thought, "There's some mystery here and we'll find out what it is."

CHAPTER SEVEN

GHOST PONY

"YOU must have imagined it all," Lucy said, "or dreamed it."

"We jolly well didn't. We both heard it absolutely as clearly as anything," Jonathan retorted.

They were having breakfast in the caravan. Debbie scooped some marmalade on to a chunk of bread with her knife. "Could he have got into a garden at the end of the village?" she suggested. "And that's why you suddenly didn't hear him anymore."

"Could be," Mark agreed. "We'll ask Mr. Appleton if anyone's missed a pony."

Just then Mrs. Appleton appeared at the cottage door and began to shake a rug. Lucy and Debbie ran across to ask her where they could buy milk.

She told them and then asked if they'd slept well.

"We did, thanks," Lucy answered. "But the boys were woken up by a horse going down the road and they thought it must be one of ours so they got up and went after it."

"But they couldn't find it," Debbie joined in.

Mrs. Appleton's cheerful face changed rather suddenly and she looked almost worried. "Oh. Well—if I was you I wouldn't go out at night if you hear summat. And best tell your brothers not to neither."

"Why?" Lucy asked.

"Well, 'tis nothing." Mrs. Appleton hesitated. "But best stay in o' night," she said vaguely.

"But why? What happens?" Debbie's curiosity was aroused.

" 'Tis unlucky, they do say. Just an old tale," Mrs. Appleton said. "Maybe I shouldn't have said anything."

"Now you have you must tell us everything," Lucy said.

"Yes do," Debbie urged. "Or we'll never stop wondering about it."

"Come on, Mrs. Appleton, in the caravan—and have a cup of tea," Lucy said coaxingly. "We've only just finished breakfast and there's plenty left."

Mrs. Appleton allowed herself to be persuaded to climb the steps into the caravan where she was settled in a chair.

"She's going to tell us something exciting about hearing that horse last night," Debbie told the boys.

Lucy poured tea into a mug with pink roses on it. "Sugar? Two lumps?"

Mrs. Appleton accepted it and then admired the caravan, and the girls were glad that they'd made their beds. Mark and Jonathan sat on the spare bunk as there were only four chairs. Now it was not in use Mrs. Manning's bunk was a convenient place for putting things, and it was covered with Lucy's and Debbie's clothes, a shopping basket, the bridles and some books. The boys perched on top of everything with Locket between them curled up on a jersey of Lucy's.

"What is all this?" Mark asked. "Did you hear a horse too, Mrs. Appleton?"

She looked round. "I don't know as I ought—I don't want to scare you but 'tis for your own good."

"Do tell," Lucy begged.

"We're dying of curiosity," Debbie said.

" 'Tis like this. When we hears a horse going down the road at night we don't look out. 'Tis terrible bad luck to see aught."

"A ghost!" Lucy burst out. "How thrilling! I've always wanted to see one."

"Same here," said Jonathan. "Not that I believe in them, only if there is one I'd like to see it."

"I wouldn't," Debbie said.

"There's no need to be scared," Mrs. Appleton said comfortably. "If you stays in no harm'll come to you. There's not a soul in Kensleigh as 'ud go out when they heard a horse at night."

"Why? What's the story?" asked Mark.

Mrs. Appleton settled herself comfortably against the cushions in her chair and Lucy refilled her cup to encourage her. In her soft voice with its pleasant country accent she told them the story.

"Several hundred years ago the Kensleighs lived at Kensleigh Hall, down at the bottom of the hill it was. Lord Kensleigh had a son, Lord Charles, and a little girl, Lady Jane. She was a good bit younger than her brother but she was special fond of him, it seems. The family were on bad terms with another family in the neighbourhood. The Wicked Merrylls they were called and there'd been bad blood atween the families for years."

"A feud!" Lucy exclaimed delightedly. "How thrilling!"

"Shut up, Lucy," said Jonathan. "Go on, please, Mrs. Appleton."

"It seems that the Merrylls planned to murder Lord Charles," Mrs. Appleton continued, "as he was coming home from some party or such-like. They were to lie in wait but Jane, only ten or eleven she were, found out and rode to meet him to warn him. A white pony, it were."

Debbie was leaning forward with her elbows on her knees and her chin in her hands, gazing at Mrs. Appleton.

"Seems as if her brother came back early, she was too late to warn him, any road. The little girl came up just as they'd struck him down and she turned to ride home but the Wicked Merrylls went after and killed her too—so she shouldn't say what she'd seen."

"Beasts!" said Debbie fiercely.

"In those bad old days folks weren't over particular how many they killed," Mrs. Appleton said.

"Who's the ghost?" Jonathan demanded. "Lady Jane rides again?"

"Why no, 'tis the pony. It went home without her and on these nights, generally when th' moon's full, it trots back to Kensleigh Hall same as it did that night."

"Honestly?" Lucy asked. "I mean, have real

people seen it now, and not just old people hundreds of years ago?"

"My father used to tell me of people who'd seen it," Mrs. Appleton said. "But it do bring terrible bad luck. Nobody 'ud look out when they heard horse hooves in the road of a night, not for anything."

"Who has seen it and had bad luck?" Mark asked. "Anyone lately?"

Mrs. Appleton considered and then replied, "My father's uncle saw it, clear as anything in the moonlight, a white pony with a saddle and no one riding it, trotting down the road it were. Next day he fell off a ladder and broke his leg."

"Tough luck!" Mark said.

"And me husband's grandfather told of a man who saw it and took the smallpox and died."

"Golly!" said Debbie. "I shan't look out for it."

"That's real sensible," Mrs. Appleton said approvingly. "No good comes of it, any road."

"Is it often heard?" Mark asked.

"Not reg'lar like," Mrs. Appleton answered. "It's not been about for ever so long until just lately. There's been talk of folks hearing it these last two or three weeks, and th' moon's full now."

"It was bright last night," said Jonathan.

Mrs. Appleton got up and thanked Lucy for the tea. "I must be getting along. There's the Sunday dinner to cook."

"Thank you awfully for telling us about it," Lucy said. "I do hope I see the ghost because I've always simply longed to see one. I'll even risk breaking my leg. I shan't get smallpox as I've been vaccinated."

"Don't you joke about it," Mrs. Appleton said seriously. "There's been sad things happen after anyone seen the White Pony. You stay in like a sensible girl."

"I shall," said Debbie. "I'd be scared stiff of a ghost."

Mrs. Appleton went back to her cottage. They watched her pick up the rug she had been shaking and then go indoors. They looked at each other expectantly. This was going to be exciting.

"How smashing! A ghost!" Lucy gloated. "We must see it."

"I shan't look," Debbie said determinedly.

"I will," said Jonathan. "We'll watch for it, won't we, Mark?"

He didn't answer. He was sitting staring out of the door and frowning hard.

"Don't you believe in it, Mark?" asked Lucy.

"Yes, in a way. That story must be true though it's probably been exaggerated over the years. The village people here have grown up hearing it so they believe it, but I just can't see it happening now."

"Ghosts do," Lucy persisted. "I've heard haunted houses described on the radio."

"Sometimes," Mark agreed. "I don't know—I'll believe in it when I see it. There's something in it but I can't think what it is."

"The bad luck!" Debbie exclaimed.

"Just coincidence," Mark assured her. "That chap would have fallen off the ladder anyhow, and the old boy would have got smallpox just the same, ghost or no ghost. Smallpox was a very common disease and there was no cure, hundreds of people died of it."

"I thought last night there was a mystery," Jonathan said.

"I think there is too," Mark said, "and it's tied up with this ghost yarn in some way. Remember that odd noise we heard when we were coming back from the field?"

"A ghost chariot?" Jonathan giggled.

"It wasn't supernatural," Mark said. "It was something whizzing down the hill and I can't think what or why. Do you know what the time was when we first heard the hooves, Jon?"

"I'm not sure, but it was one o'clock when we were at the field because I looked at my watch in the moonlight."

"We were at least half an hour getting into our clothes and then walking along the road looking for a horse," Mark said thoughtfully. "Okay, we'll start to watch for it at midnight."

"Smashing!" Lucy said. "I say, Deb, would you stay in the caravan with Locket? I don't want to take her and she'd be happier with you than alone."

" 'Fraid she'll see the ghost pony and get distemper?" asked Jonathan teasingly.

"Of course not, you idiot," Lucy said.

"I think I'll come," Debbie said. "I shouldn't be scared of a *pony* ghost, nobody could be. And I shan't mind if we're all together, people generally seem to be alone when frightening things happen, at least they do in books."

"I suppose there isn't an alarm clock?" Mark asked. "We'll never stay awake, but if we go to sleep I don't know how we're going to wake up at the right time."

"I can," Debbie said. "I always wake up when I want to by banging my head on the end of the bed the number of hours for the time I want to wake."

"Eleven-thirty. Eleven and a half bangs," Mark said. "Your poor old head, Debbie!"

"Quite little bangs will do," she said. "We've got to ring Mummie, we'd better do it now."

"We'll do it on the way as we fetch the milk," said Jonathan. "Coming, Mark?"

The boys went off with the milk cans, and Lucy and Debbie began to look through the supply of tinned food and to plan a meal for midday.

"If we don't see the ghost pony tonight we'll have to think up a really marvellous excuse for staying on here," Lucy said, putting aside a big tin of sausages, "because I couldn't bear to leave without seeing the White Pony."

CHAPTER EIGHT

THE GREAT PONY MYSTERY

"... NINE ... ten ... eleven ... and a half." Debbie was bumping her head gently against the end of her bunk.

"Does it really make you wake up when you want to?" Lucy asked.

"Yes, it always works. But I wake very easily and that may make a difference."

It was quite early, but they were going to bed so as to get some sleep before turning out to watch for the ghost pony.

"I'll try it too," and Lucy bumped her head eleven times, and one little bump for the half hour.

They lay down on their bunk-beds wearing their clothes and with their shoes and an extra jersey put ready to slip on quickly. They watched the light outside fading and then the grey patch, which was the open top half of the door, get darker and darker.

"I hope there's a bright moon again tonight because the torch battery's awfully feeble," Debbie said. "We must buy a new one at the first shop we see."

"Deb, do you think Aunt Di would let us stay here another night?"

"She might as we're getting on all right," Debbie answered. "Shoeing Ajax will take all the morning, so we might as well stay till next day."

"The ghost may not appear again for quite a long while," Lucy sighed. "I wish I could go to sleep quickly or it'll be time to wake up again at once." She yawned and turned over, cuddling Locket, and presently she slept.

Debbie woke her, only a few minutes later it seemed to Lucy, saying, "It's half-past eleven. Hurry."

"The trick worked then? It didn't for me but I knew it wouldn't." Lucy sat up rubbing her eyes. She longed to lie down and sleep again but the hope of seeing the White Pony made her struggle up and she began to grope for her shoes.

"Well, I've woken up several times," Debbie admitted. "The last time was at five to eleven so I stayed awake to make sure. I'll chase up the boys."

As Lucy pulled on her thick jersey she heard voices from the tent and then Debbie came back. "The grass is sopping with dew, we'd better wear wellies."

They hunted for and found them by the dim light of the torch. Then Lucy tucked Locket up cosily and told her she'd soon be back and they went out, shutting the caravan door behind them.

Jonathan was fastening Tiger's chain to the tent pole. "If he pulls hard he'll have it down but it was all right last night. Stay Tiger, good dog, stay there."

"Don't make a row," Mark said in a low voice.

"Are ghosts scared away by people?" Debbie asked. "I thought it was the other way round."

"There may be someone else about besides the

ghost," Mark said, "that odd noise we heard, like wheels, must have had somebody with it because I'm sure it wasn't anything spooky."

"I'm not," Jonathan said, "I think it might have been anything. Jolly mysterious, anyway."

"Where are we going to watch?" Lucy asked.

"At the entrance to this lane. We can keep in the shadow of the houses and still see up the village street." Mark said. "Come on. Operation Ghost-hunt begins!"

Then Debbie clutched Mark's arm. "It's come!"

They all heard it. A pony was trotting down the road. It was quite distinct and it was coming nearer. For a moment they all stood still, too surprised to move. Then Jonathan exclaimed, "Come on!" and began to run towards the gate.

"Quietly," hissed Mark.

"No, don't scare it away before we've seen it," Lucy whispered.

It took several minutes to climb the gate and then run, as quietly but as quickly as possible, up the short lane from the forge to the road. All this time they could hear the clip-clop of the pony.

"It's not much further away," muttered Lucy, "it won't be gone before we see it."

But before they reached the road the sounds stopped. They crept cautiously into the road and looked up and down the village street. No White Pony—nothing. Debbie, who had forgotten she'd meant to keep her eyes shut if it came, was relieved but a tiny bit disappointed too. It would've been marvellous to be able to say you'd seen a ghost, and a pony ghost was a nice sort of ghost.

"Sickening," Lucy was saying, quite crossly.

"Mouldy luck!" Jonathan agreed. "We almost saw it."

"Almost," Mark agreed. "Keep back in the shadows."

The moonlight was as bright as day. The houses on the far side of the street looked white, so did the road, and the shadows on the side where the children stood were like black velvet.

"Why keep back? There's nobody about," Jonathan remarked.

"I'm not sure I didn't see someone disappear in the shadows down at the end there, by the last house. He could've got into a garden. But I couldn't be certain," Mark explained, speaking softly.

"So what?" asked Jonathan.

"So he was the chap who was the ghost," Mark said. "I thought it didn't sound quite right but I can't say why—there was just something."

"It was exactly like a pony going along a road," Lucy protested, "with that rather hollow sound of echoing between the houses."

"That's it," Mark exclaimed. "That hollow sound. I knew something didn't sound right—it was too hollow."

"I thought it was just like a pony," Debbie said.

"Maybe I'm wrong," said Mark. "Keep in the shadows and we'll wait and see if there's anything else happening tonight."

"What could be?" Jonathan asked. "The chariot?"

"Pr'aps. I'd like to see if it comes. I've got an

idea this isn't on the level, but I can't see how or why."

"About half an hour to wait," Jonathan yawned.

"You all go back to bed," Mark suggested.

"Not likely, I mean to be here if anything happens," Jonathan said fervently.

"Me too," said Lucy. "The ghost pony might come back."

Debbie didn't want to go back alone, anyway now she came to think about it she hadn't been one bit scared when they heard the ghost pony. If it was true it was terribly sad, and Lady Jane had been awfully brave.

They leaned against the wall of one of the cottages at the end of the lane. Nothing is so boring as waiting and it's worse if you're sleepy. Only obstinacy kept Jonathan and Lucy from going back to bed. Debbie waited because they did. Mark was convinced there was something worth waiting for—some solution to the mystery.

The wall was rough and the nobbles wore into their shoulders as they leaned against it. They were hardly able to see each other in the blackness of the shadows, yet across the road, in full moonlight, the houses looked satin-white.

"Let's pack it in," Jonathan suggested, changing his position to find a smoother bit of wall. "Nothing's happening."

"You go," Mark said softly. "I'll hang on for a bit."

"Surely it would've come by now if it was coming," Lucy whispered. There was something about the night which made one want to whisper and to keep in the shadows. Waiting for something was a jumpy business at midnight.

"I reckoned it was half an hour after the trotting sounds, last night," Mark said.

"What do you think it really was?" Debbie asked. She had a great admiration for Mark's ideas as they usually turned out well.

"I haven't a clue," he answered, "only I think something odd's going on."

"Shall we go back, Lucy?" Debbie asked. The thought of snuggling down in bed was very tempting.

Lucy thought so too, and Locket would be pleased when she came back to her. "All right. It does seem as though nothing else'll happen. And we did hear the ghost even if we didn't see it."

"Mrs. Appleton will be glad we didn't," Debbie said. "Do you think we can count it as a ghost?"

"Of course, we heard it and it wasn't there so it was a ghost," Jonathan gave a great yawn.

"Push off to bed, I'll be along soon," Mark said.

"Okay," said Jonathan.

"Sh!" Mark whispered suddenly. "I think I heard something, a sort of thud."

The night was very still and every sound carried. Listening their hardest they heard a clink as if metal clashed against metal and then a thump. Was it a man's voice muttering something? Easy to imagine things, Lucy thought, but then there was another thud. Someone was moving things, she decided, heavy things.

"They're up the village," Mark whispered, "not far, 'bout half way."

"What is there? Ponies' field. Above that the church," Jonathan said. "Nothing else save cottages. Pr'aps they're burgling a house and carrying stuff out."

"Something like that," Mark murmured.

"Could we sneak along in the shadows and see——" Jonathan began.

"Sh!" Mark hissed. "It's coming. Keep still."

They cowered against the wall in the darkness and watched the strip of moonlit road in front of them.

"Here it comes," whispered Mark.

The swishing sound was coming down the hill and getting nearer rapidly. There was a little indistinct rattle and Mark muttered, "A car, I thought so."

It passed across the opening and was only in view for a flash but they saw quite clearly a car with a truck body—and then it was gone.

Mark and Jonathan ran into the road and watched it disappearing into the distance. Then they rejoined the girls. As they did so they heard a car engine.

"He's switched on now, the hill takes him well out of the village," Mark said.

"Did you get the number?" asked Jonathan. "I couldn't see it."

"He wasn't using any lights so the number plates didn't show," Mark explained.

"What's it mean?" Lucy asked.

"I'm not sure how it ties up with the ghost," Mark said thoughtfully. "Definitely dirty work though."

"And now we can go back to bed," said Debbie. They climbed the gate into the orchard because it was stiff and the hinges creaked when it was opened. Mark, a farmer's son, told them it was bad for gates to be climbed as it weakened the hinges and strained it. Climbing it the end near the hinges did least damage, he said, but they were too sleepy to care.

"We heard the ghost, anyway," Lucy said, as they parted to go to the caravan.

"And we saw a pick-up," Mark said. "That truck, I mean. Wish we could've got the number."

Lucy and Debbie crept up the steps into the caravan where Locket welcomed Lucy joyfully.

"It's been terrifically exciting. Locket, don't lick my nose, please!" Lucy said, crawling into bed.

CHAPTER NINE

"*WHY COCONUTS*?"

IT WAS eight o'clock before anyone woke next morning and so breakfast was very late. The cooks jibbed at cooking and served cornflakes and then sardines laid on thick slices of bread. Mark was afraid that Mr. Appleton would be waiting for them to bring Ajax to be shod so he hurried over his breakfast.

"No need for you all to rush," he said, bolting his cornflakes, "I'll fetch him." And he seized a slab of bread and sardine and dashed off to the field.

"We simply *can't* leave here today," Jonathan said. "It'd be awful to have to go away without solving this supersonic, gigantic mystery."

"Specially as we might solve it tonight if we could stay," Lucy chimed in, giving a little taste of sardine to Locket who was on her lap.

"I want to see Ajax shod," Debbie said. She didn't mind so much about the mystery, though it'd be nice to know the reason for these strange goings-on, and she'd rather not see a ghost but she enjoyed seeing horses shod.

"Me too," said Jonathan. "If this Appleton bloke's a decent type he may let us work the bellows."

Lucy filled up their teacups, it was a good reason for putting off clearing away and washing up. Then there were the beds to make—and the midday meal to prepare. Thank goodness for all those tins.

"Do you think Mummie'd let us stay another night if we just say we want to?" Jonathan asked. "It'd be so difficult to tell her everything, the ghost story and the truck and all, over the 'phone."

"And she mightn't approve of us getting up in the night," said Debbie, who'd had doubts about this.

"She'd be sure to think we were getting tired," Lucy remarked.

"Are you tired, Lucy?" Debbie asked anxiously, her conscience reminding her that Lucy mustn't do too much.

"Not a bit," she answered cheerfully. "After all, we have pretty lazy days, just sitting around most of the time. I feel terribly well."

"Oh good!" Debbie said. "*Don't* go and get tired."

"Here are Mark and Ajax," Jonathan said, and they all went across to the forge where Mr. Appleton met them and led Ajax in, tying him to an iron ring in the wall. He wore his leather apron and his box of tools stood ready. A bright fire was glowing and sending out sparks and the smithy had a peculiar smell of smoke and horse hoof.

"Will he need more than the two front shoes?" Lucy asked. She was wondering if they'd have enough money if he had to be shod all round. She was good at mathematics and businesslike with money, so Mrs. Manning had given her the funds to look after. Debbie was hopeless at mathematics and bad at counting her change.

Mr. Appleton picked up each of Ajax's huge feet in turn. Then he stood up and pushed back his cap to rub his head. "He'll have to have both front 'uns new. His hind shoes are thin, worse'n I thought when I seed 'em last night." He looked at them again. "Best have new or he'll be casting one afore long."

"Okay," Mark said. "We don't want him to hold us up again by losing a shoe. We mightn't be so lucky finding a blacksmith next time."

" 'Deed you wouldn't," Mr. Appleton said. "I don't know of another shoeing smith for twenty miles. Repair farm implements but not shoe a horse."

"It'll take a good time to shoe him, won't it?" Jonathan asked.

"Get it done by midday if I've the material," Mr. Appleton replied. "I'll have to make the shoes, I've none big enough. Ponies and hunters come in regular-like but I don't often shoe a cart horse."

He went to the far end of the smithy and began to pull some long metal bars from a rack. He put them all back and came back to the children and Ajax.

"I've nothing heavy enough." He pushed his cap back even further so that Debbie wondered if it would fall off. "I can get it here soon after dinner time and have him ready roundabout five." He looked at Mark. "Bit late for starting off. Could you stay another night?"

"Rather! You bet we will," Jonathan said delightedly.

"It looks as though we must." Mark grinned at

Mr. Appleton who laughed and said, "It do, don't it!"

"How much will it cost?" Lucy asked, and they sighed with relief when he told them for they could pay it and still have a little money left. Mr. Appleton said he'd start shoeing directly the iron came and then he'd be sure of having him ready for them that evening. Mark led Ajax back to the field and Jonathan said he'd telephone to Mrs. Manning. He felt in his jeans pockets—"No cash."

"There's some coppers in the funds," Lucy said. She kept the money in a purse lent her by Mrs. Manning. "Let's all go and we can fetch some milk."

They collected the big milk-can and walked up the village to the telephone-box outside the Post Office.

Mrs. Manning wasn't a worrying kind of person and she didn't sound anxious on hearing they would have to stay another night. She asked if they were all well and had enough money. Then she reminded them they were only six miles away and Mrs. Thursby would drive her over if they were in any difficulty. They must come tomorrow, she added, as they only had the caravan for another three days. She had finished the pictures of Midget and Brandy and Mrs. Thursby was very pleased with them. And were they all really all right?

"We're all okay," Debbie answered, "and we've enough money to pay for Ajax's shoes. We've not spent much as we're using all those tins."

"Nothing but tinned food's not good for you,"

Mrs. Manning said. "You need fresh vegetables and fruit and proper meals."

"Our meals are proper," Debbie protested. "Lucy's awfully good at it."

"You're not letting her get over-tired? Don't do anything silly."

"No, Mummie." Then someone else came to use the telephone and looked so impatient that Debbie rang off. Her conscience was woken up again by her mother's remark. She'd think it silly to get up in the night when Lucy mustn't tire herself, but Debbie couldn't say anything because Lucy was touchy about not being able to do as much as everyone else. Perhaps if Debbie spent the afternoon reading Lucy would too, if she rested it wouldn't matter going out at night.

The farm which sold milk was at the top of the village. Looking down they could see the straight road which stretched away from the bottom of the hill, and they could see a bit of the caravan's roof among the trees in the orchard.

"They've got a tough-looking dog here," Jonathan told the girls. "Better stay out here with Tiger and Locket."

So they waited in the road while Jonathan went in to buy milk. On the other side of the road a car was standing, it had an open truck body, like a small lorry, and was very old and battered. Two youths were lolling against it and they strolled across and pretended to admire Locket.

"Cor, jus' like a woolly mat!" The speaker was a ginger-haired boy in a bright red pullover. Not a good colour scheme, Debbie thought.

"Is 'e for sale?" the other youth asked. He was a little older and taller, wearing a black leather jacket and tight black jeans. "I know someone as wants a dawg like that. Give yer a fiver for 'im."

"She's not for sale," Lucy declared indignantly. The idea—selling Locket! "And she's worth lots more than five pounds."

"What'll ye take? It'd be a good 'ome," the black-jacketted youth asked.

The ginger-haired boy giggled and said something they didn't catch. Then he stooped and snapped his fingers at Locket. "Come on, pooch!"

Lucy snatched her up and clasped her tightly. Tiger walked forward growling. His hair was bristling and his growl was deep-throated and sounded fierce.

The youths fell back towards the truck.

"All right, Tiger." Debbie held his collar but he went on growling, and the youths got into the truck, the older one in the driving seat.

"Jon," Debbie said, as he joined them. "Is that the sort of car that Mark called a pick-up last night?"

"Yes. Tough sort of guys." They watched as the truck went down the village street. Jonathan noted the number but, he said, pick-ups were very common.

"I wish I hadn't said Locket was worth more than five pounds," Lucy said. "Suppose they try to steal her?"

"I don't suppose we'll see them again," Debbie said, "and Tiger wouldn't let them. I've never heard him growl so loudly."

"Good for him," Jonathan said when they told him how the youths had been teasing them.

On the way back they turned off to visit the ponies who came up to the gate with hopefully out-stretched noses.

"But all we've got are crumbs," Debbie said sadly, turning out her jacket pockets and only finding some messy crumbly sugar lumps, a stray oat or two and tiny scraps of bread. Puck liked bread and she usually took a crust when she went to catch him. They took the crumbly fragments from her flat palm with their soft lips and blew warmly as they nuzzled.

"We might ride this afternoon," Jonathan suggested.

"Ajax is being shod," Debbie reminded him.

"It'll take ages, plenty of time to watch for a bit and ride."

The breakfast things were still waiting to be cleared away and washed so they went on down the hill and along the little lane to the forge.

Mr. Appleton was talking to a clergyman. He was just leaving but he stopped to speak to the children. He was elderly with white hair and a round, pink face; his pale blue eyes had a twinkle lurking in them.

"So you're the gypsies?" he asked. "Appleton told me he had visitors. Your horse chose a good place to lose his shoe. George Appleton's a first-class smith and a very nice fellow."

"We were lucky." Lucy nodded, and Debbie envied the easy way she could talk to strangers.

He admired Locket and told Lucy that Yorkies

were one of the most intelligent breeds, his mother had had one years ago and he'd never forgotten how clever it was. Then he asked about Tiger. Was he a Boxer, and did he fight at all? And Debbie found herself telling him about all the animals she'd left at home.

"Do you live here?" Lucy asked, because they hadn't seen a house which looked like a vicarage.

"No, Kensleigh is too small to be a parish on its own, so it goes with two others, and I live at the largest."

"It's a sweet little village," Debbie said, "with all the little thatched cottages."

"A dear little place," the Vicar agreed, "and we have a lovely little church, very old, but we have grave difficulties in keeping it up with such a small congregation and repairs so expensive."

"We do too," Lucy told him, "our church tower is always getting up something to stop it falling down."

"Does it give dances?" Jonathan asked, and Lucy said he knew quite well what she meant.

"I must go as I've people to visit," the Vicar said. "Goodbye and good luck with your journeying. I hope you will find your animal family thriving when you get home," he told Debbie.

They said goodbye and then set about the belated washing up.

"Wasn't he nice!" Debbie remarked. "Can I wash while you dry, Lucy? Jonathan could fill the oil-stove, it's getting low. Outside the caravan, Jon, in case you spill any and then it might get set alight."

After they had finished lunch Jonathan suggested going for a ride. "Coming, Deb?" he asked.

"You and Mark ride, I don't want to."

The boys went to bring Ajax to the forge and the ponies to the caravan to be saddled. After that they went out for a ride to explore the country round Kensleigh.

Debbie settled down on her bed with a book, the first opportunity for a good read since they'd been in the caravan. Lucy stretched out on her bunk with Locket curled up beside her and they read in silence.

Presently Debbie found herself dozing and she let go of her book and drifted into sleep. When she woke she raised herself on her elbow and looked across at Lucy. She was lying on her side and Debbie couldn't see her face, but she was so still that she was certain she was asleep. Debbie felt heavy and only half-awake, but she got up and crept out of the caravan carrying her shoes.

At the bottom of the steps she put them on and looked at her watch. She could only have slept for a very short time, but perhaps Lucy would sleep longer. Now she was in the fresh air she became wide-awake and felt very refreshed, so even a little sleep was worth while.

She went across to the forge and stood beside Ajax while Mr. Appleton fitted a shoe on a hind foot. Ajax stood like a rock.

"I can't think how they put up with it when it sizzles," Debbie said.

Mr. Appleton carried the shoe back to the fire where he heated it again, holding it in long pincers, then he plunged it into water and it hissed loudly.

"Get used to it," he said. "There's a lot in how they're handled first time they're shod—fright 'em and they don't forget that."

Debbie stayed to watch, occasionally helping by holding Ajax or blowing up the fire (Mr. Appleton said she was a great help). Presently Lucy joined her looking flushed and sleepy but she said she'd had a marvellous sleep and was all ready for the night.

Meanwhile Mark and Jonathan were riding along lanes which, Jonathan said with his usual optimism and faith in his map-reading, would take them round in a half-circle and bring them back to Kensleigh at the top of the village.

They had started out along the downhill road and had noticed that it went on down gradually for quite a long way, and Mark pointed out that the man in the pick-up wouldn't have to use his engine till he was clear of the village.

They looked for any signs of the ruins of Kensleigh Hall, but they found nothing to show where it had stood.

"Do you believe in the ghost story?" Jonathan asked.

"Not really. I know some people see ghosts and make it sound convincing, but I always think they must imagine it because they want to see them."

"It'd be super to be able to say you'd really seen one. The chaps at school'd be mad with envy," Jonathan said.

"If they believed you," Mark said with his grin.

They trotted on, Mark on Kit-Kat because he

was the tallest and heaviest and Kit-Kat was the biggest pony. He was a lovely ride, as he was so quick to answer to the Aids and so eager, but Jonathan liked riding Puck, for the roan was comfortable and had such a kind, wise temperament.

Soon they came to a fork in the lane where, in between the fork where the road divided, there was a small field stacked with heaps of metal, several old cars, piles of worn-out tyres, tin baths, oil-drums, sheets of corrugated tin—every kind of old metal.

"Look at that junk. What a mess!" Jonathan said.

"A scrap dealer's yard. Amazing how you find them everywhere," Mark commented.

"And there's the pick-up we saw in the village with the two toughs who were seen off by Tiger." Jonathan pointed to a shabby truck standing at the gate into the field.

The lane was narrow, so Mark pulled Kit-Kat back behind Puck and they walked by in single file. Looking down at the pick-up as he passed he saw something lying in the driver's seat.

He gave a little whistle and stopped so that he could lean down and look right into the front of the truck.

"What's up?" Jonathan asked, turning in his saddle to look back.

Mark rode on and came up beside him. He was frowning in a puzzled way. "What'd you use a coconut for, Jon? When it's empty, I mean."

"I haven't a clue. Don't people get milk out of them?"

"After they're empty, I mean," Mark repeated patiently. "I know there's something they're used for but I can't remember what it is. There are two in that pick-up. Funny things to carry round. What a clot I am not to remember."

Mark was very silent riding home. Jonathan gave up trying to talk. Old Mark was broody about coconuts and he wouldn't be any fun till he got over it.

CHAPTER TEN

THE PLAN

THE BOYS got back in time to help put on Ajax's last shoe. Then Mark climbed on to his broad back to take him up to the field and Jonathan followed, riding Kit-Kat bare-back and leading Puck; the saddles having been left at the caravan.

"We said we'd ring Mummie and tell her when Ajax was definitely ready," Debbie remembered. "I'll go and do it now."

Lucy gave her some change and she went to the telephone-box outside the Post Office. Her mother was relieved to hear that they would be coming back next day. She'd be glad to see them all again, she said, and it would be cutting it rather fine to get the caravan back on time if they delayed any more. "See you tomorrow, darling, and love to everyone."

" 'Bye." Debbie replaced the receiver and lingered in the telephone-box. It was hot and airless, untidy with empty cigarette packets and toffee papers, but she didn't notice any of this. She'd been thinking a lot about her animals at home and she suddenly felt she *had* to know if they were all right. Lucy'd said they were running out of money, but a few pence couldn't make any difference, and they'd be joining Mummie tomorrow and she'd pay for things then.

Debbie dialled and inserted pennies—a lot of pennies—and then Mrs. Bristow's voice said, "Hallo. Who is it speaking? Oh, Deborah!" She was one of the few people who called Debbie this, mostly it was only used at school on Reports and Lists.

"Could I speak to Tim please, Mrs. Bristow?"

"I'll call him."

Debbie waited anxiously. What was Tim going to tell her about the animals? And she'd no more pennies if he was ages coming——

" 'Lo, Deb!" Tim's voice was beginning to break and this was one of it's squeaky days.

"How are they all?" Debbie asked breathlessly.

"Fine. 'Cept for that titchy little guinea-pig. 'Fraid he's had it. Passed away. Sorry about that but everything else is okay."

"It doesn't matter much," Debbie was able to say truthfully. "I thought he might. Is Snoozy well?"

"He's fine, very sleepy. Cats are okay, and Hammish and Wiggs—the lot. All jolly fine."

"Thanks awfully, Tim. We'll be back——" The pips broke in before she could finish.

She skipped joyfully down the road. That poor little guinea-pig had been a weak one that she'd not expected to rear so she hadn't given it a name. The others were all fine. Good old Tim. She bounded up the caravan steps

"The change, please," said Lucy.

Debbie handed it over.

"Is this all? Gosh, you must've paid double. Or did you go on talking for hours after the pips?"

"There aren't pips ringing to Mrs. Thursby's," Mark said. "It's a local call."

Debbie said guiltily that she'd rung Tim.

"*Honestly!*" Lucy said. "When we're short of cash."

"I had to know how the animals were," Debbie pleaded.

"But we'll be home in three days," Mark said.

"I know. But I just had to."

"Of all the dim-witted girls," Jonathan grumbled. "Now we'll starve tomorrow."

"Sorry," Debbie said. "Shall we really, Lucy?"

"We've hardly any money left after paying for Ajax," Lucy replied. "We shan't have enough to buy milk and bread tomorrow. And there aren't many tins left."

"I'm not surprised—the rate we've been opening them," Mark remarked. "Let's have supper straight away then we can have a good shut-eye before tonight."

"Sleep? Now?" asked Jonathan.

"Sure. Nobody can keep going day and night, we need a sleep before we go out."

"Mark's so sensible!" said Jonathan, and Mark grinned and asked what was wrong with a bit of sense?

"Actually, Lucy and I slept this afternoon," Debbie said.

"Good for you," Mark commented.

Debbie took Ajax's bridle off her bed and dropped it on the spare bunk (they'd have to tidy it up before Mummie could use it again), and said Mark wasn't the only one with sense. She was feeling particularly happy. The animals were all right, except for the smallest guinea-pig and that hadn't been unexpected, and her conscience wasn't bothering her. She'd decided it wasn't wrong to go out at night, in fact she could imagine her mother leading a party to investigate the ghost pony story. It would only matter if they got over-tired, specially Lucy, but as she'd slept that didn't count.

They opened the last tins of spaghetti in tomato sauce for supper. Lucy grated the end of the cheese to sprinkle over it and said it was a pity they'd no eggs as they'd have been good with it, fried or poached.

It was when they were finishing their meal with bananas and biscuits (the last of both) that Mark suddenly burst out, "I've got it! Coconut shells. Horses' hooves."

"*What?*" Debbie asked, mystified.

He explained about seeing coconut shells in the pick-up. "I couldn't remember what people use them for and Jon didn't know. It's for making a noise like horse hooves going along a road. They use them on TV and radio."

"I know," Lucy said calmly. "We did a play at school and they came in Noises Off. A girl called Melanie Purkiss did it frightfully well."

"Crikey! You knew all the time," Mark said, "and I was wearing out my brain trying to remember."

"But why?" asked Debbie.

"Don't you see?" Mark said in an excited way that was unlike his usual slow and calm way of speaking. "Someone's doing these hoof noises to frighten everybody into staying indoors and not looking out. Remember, Mrs. Appleton said no one in Kensleigh'd risk seeing the White Pony? They're using the ghost story to get a clear run at some dirty work."

"That's pretty bright," said Jonathan.

"I knew those horse hooves didn't sound absolutely right," Mark said.

"It's a gang!" Jonathan stated. "Those two toughs are in it."

"But what are they doing?" asked Debbie.

"Burglars?" Lucy suggested.

"Stealing something and taking it away in that pick-up. Nobody will look out and see 'cos they're scared of the ghost," Jonathan said, "and it goes down the hill and out of the village without the engine so nobody hears it."

"What are they stealing?" Mark said slowly. "That's what I can't make out. There's no house big enough to be worth while, and anyway it can't be an ordinary burglary or they wouldn't come back the next night."

They were all silent while they thought about this and Jonathan murmured "Not an ordinary house."

"There's only the church," Debbie began, and Mark interrupted her.

"The church. That's where they start from. They're taking something from the church—something that's pretty bulky as it takes several nights to get it."

"And as the Vicar has three parishes to look

after he won't be here often or have many services," Lucy said, "so whatever they're doing won't be noticed. But what can it be?"

"Stealing the bells?" Debbie suggested.

"Too heavy," Jonathan said. "They weigh a ton or more."

"I've got it, I think," said Mark. "It's lead from the roof, and they're selling it to that scrap merchant."

"I bet that's it," Jonathan agreed. "Good for you, Mark."

"I took the heck of a time to think of it," Mark said, "and the coconut shells too. I'm pretty dim."

"Why lead?" Debbie asked.

"Lots of church roofs have lead on them and it's terribly expensive stuff," Mark explained. "And fairly easy to rip off, I guess."

"When it rains they'll find it's gone," Jonathan giggled. "Blimey! All their Sunday hat's'll get wet unless they've umbrellas."

"It's not funny, Jon," Debbie said sternly. "It's awfully wrong to steal from a church, and that poor old clergyman——"

"Goodness yes," Lucy said. "He's got money troubles already. If he has to re-roof the church it'll be the absolute end."

"And he's so nice," Debbie said. He'd really seemed to understand how she felt about all her animals left at home.

"Jolly nice," Lucy agreed. "He knows Yorkies aren't just silly little lap-dogs but clever and tough."

"That's nothing to do with this gang stealing

the lead," Mark said impatiently. "We've got to think up a way of stopping them."

"Catching 'em at it," said Jonathan.

"That'd be best," Mark nodded. "And get back what they've taken."

"Shall we tell the Vicar?" Lucy suggested. "Mrs. Appleton would tell us where he lives."

Mark looked doubtful. "We've no proof, it's only guesswork and we could be wrong."

"Let's watch and catch 'em at it," Jonathan said.

"We'll watch," Mark agreed. "As soon as we know what they're doing we'll 'phone the police and leave it to them."

"Plans," Lucy said. "It must all be planned so we don't bish it."

"We must watch the church, be there in hiding by half-past eleven," Mark said.

"I wonder if we'll see the man doing the coconut shells," Debbie said. "It sounded as though he went down the hill."

"He slinks down in the shadow and then gets into one of the gardens at the end of the village. I thought I just saw him," Mark said, "but I wasn't sure."

"Do you suppose the scrap dealer's in it too?" Jonathan asked.

"Sure, he must know it's stolen if it's brought at night," Mark answered, "and it's a crime to buy anything you know is stolen. We ought to watch his place too so we're sure it's going there. Then we can tell the cops."

"Two at the church and two at the scrap place," Jonathan suggested.

"Okay," Mark said. "Lucy and I at the church and you and Deb ride to the scrap yard. Tie up the ponies and watch to see if they bring stuff there. None of us *do* anything, simply keep out of sight and watch."

"Super! Terrific!" Jonathan said.

"I'll ring the police as soon as the pick-up leaves," Mark said. "You two come back and you can say if you saw it arrive. It's not far and you'll hear the pick-up on the road even if it doesn't go to the yard. Go past it and leave the ponies, Jon, then ride back here the way we came to the top of the village. That way you won't have to pass the scrap yard again or wait for them to go." He looked at Debbie. "Does that sound okay, Deb?"

She flushed. They'd known she was scared at going to look for the ghost so now Mark was wondering if she was scared of this. "It's smashing," she said and she meant it. Riding at night'd be fun and burglars weren't like spooks, anyway they'd be in their pick-up and she'd be on Puck.

"People will hear the ponies," Lucy said. "Some will think it's the White Pony but the gang won't."

"That's a point," said Mark thoughtfully. "I know, we'll muffle their hooves."

"Wow!" Jonathan said. "How do you do it?"

"Strips of sacking. Have we any sacks?" Mark asked.

"Tiger's biscuit meal is in a sack and it's nearly finished so we could tip it out," said Debbie. Muffled hooves at midnight! It sounded like smugglers, highwaymen, and midnight meetings on lonely heaths! Everything that was exciting. "It'll be simply thrilling!"

"Jolly exciting," Lucy said fervently. "We'll be able to watch them getting the lead. I'll leave Locket in the caravan and Tiger can guard the camp while we're away. We'd better wear our darkest clothes so we don't show up."

Mark got up. "We're using up our sleeping time. I hope they didn't finish last night. Sickening if they don't come. Can you girls do the supper things while Jon and I make muffles?"

He and Jonathan set about cutting the sack into eight pieces while Lucy and Debbie hurriedly washed up. Then they lay down on their beds. Debbie declared she could wake at eleven o'clock but it was so important that she didn't dare go to sleep, anyhow she was too excited.

In fact everyone was too excited to sleep. They dozed and then woke up with a start wondering if it was time to start yet.

CHAPTER ELEVEN

MIDNIGHT IN THE CHURCHYARD

IT WAS a dark night with a wind which blew clouds in front of the moon.

Debbie held the torch for Mark who was tying pieces of sacking over Puck's feet and cursing mildly about the torch battery which was almost useless.

"In books they say something like 'the horse's muffled hooves made no sound' but they don't tell you how to do it," Debbie observed.

"Too true! I don't know if one layer's thick enough," Mark said doubtfully. "We can't risk bodging 'em up so they might stumble, and one sack doesn't go far among eight feet."

"They'll make less noise, any road, as Mrs. Appleton says," remarked Lucy.

"Okay. That's the lot." Mark stood up and gave Puck a friendly slap. Kit-Kat had been done first. "Time you went. Keep on the grass as much as you can and keep out of sight when the gang turns up."

Debbie and Jonathan mounted and walked their ponies down the little road and out into the village street.

"They do make a little noise," Lucy said, standing still to listen.

"Not much though," Mark replied. "I can't hear them now. I hope they get past the scrap merchant's without being heard, we don't want him to get suspicious."

"Come on," Lucy said eagerly. "We must be ready when they come."

They went up the rough path behind the cottages, stumbling occasionally over stones for it was very dark.

"I'm not sure if a dark night's a help or a handicap," Mark said. "We shan't show up but it'll be difficult to see what's happening."

"Besides falling over things." Lucy tripped over something large and hard. She said a word she wasn't allowed to use and got up and followed Mark across the lane leading to the field, where Ajax was feeling a little worried at being left alone, and on up the road to the church.

The lych-gate looked black against the sky. The gate opened easily and noiselessly. Mark said, in a whisper, that they'd probably oiled it.

They tip-toed along the path between some big yew trees which had been growing since King Henry needed wood for his archers. The clouds blew from in front of the moon, and for a mere minute showed the trees, their black shadows, grey-white tombstones and the tall church tower. Then it was dark again.

Creepy, thought Lucy, Debbie would have hated it though she was as brave as anyone except with spooks. Riding through the dark to watch for a gang wasn't everyone's cup of tea—Deb was brave, all right. At this moment she bumped into Mark who had stopped.

"Look out, you ass!"

"Sorry. Why d'you have to stop suddenly?"

"Gotta find somewhere to hide. That'll do." Mark pointed towards a small wooden shed standing against the high wall which surrounded the churchyard. Its little window pane gleamed faintly and it looked lonely and deserted.

"Inside it?" Lucy asked.

"Not likely, we aren't going in anywhere we can't get out of quickly," Mark answered. "I expect it's locked. They probably keep spades for digging graves there."

"Don't!" Lucy shivered.

"Well, they must dig graves in a graveyard," Mark said reasonably as he advanced towards the hut. He flattened his nose against the window and said, "There's a mowing machine and tools for keeping the place tidy. I thought we could get behind it."

Lucy joined him, stumbling over something, she wondered if it was someone's grave, it was disrespectful to walk on them but as they were saving the church roof perhaps it didn't matter. "Horse hooves!" she said excitedly.

"Gosh yes. I'm glad they're coming. It'd have been too bad if they'd finished." Mark stood listening. "He's going down the hill. It doesn't sound absolutely right though he does it jolly well."

Lucy clutched his arm. "People," she hissed.

A man's voice was saying something very quietly but he was quite close to them. This was followed by the unmistakable noise made by a car door closing softly.

Mark pulled her back against the hut. "The

pick-up," he whispered. He felt his way along the side of the shed and found, as he had hoped, that there was a narrow space between it and the wall. They crept into this, and at that very moment the clouds cleared and the churchyard was brilliantly lit by the moon.

"Crikey!" Mark whispered, "we only just got hidden in time. The pick-up must've come very quietly, I never heard it, no engine and it's facing down hill ready to go. They're clever, this lot."

Lucy squeezed his arm "I can hear them coming," she breathed.

There were faint sounds from rubber-booted feet on the path, an unidentifiable thump and thud or two, and two men came into sight between the yew trees. They were carrying a ladder.

Lucy, craning to see, found her heart was bumping furiously. Terribly exciting, quite dangerous really, being so close to a gang of burglars—not that she'd miss it for anything.

The ladder was set up against the church and they saw the men, dark against the sky, as they mounted it.

"How long does it take to get lead off, do you suppose?" Lucy asked in a very low voice.

"Not long, it's in strips, guttering and ridges, I think," Mark answered. "It can't take long to get a load as they left about half-an-hour after the hoof noises."

The moon was darkened by cloud again, it scudded past giving intervals of light and darkness. They stood listening to faint sounds coming from the roof, clinking, taps, and sometimes a man's voice muttering something. Then there were footsteps coming up the path and the sounds on the roof stopped. A flash of a torch from the path was answered by a short stab of light from the roof.

"Don?" asked a voice softly. "Give us a 'and wi' this. Comin' down now."

"He's the chap who did the ghost pony noise," Mark whispered, "he's come to help. They're lowering something, the first lot of lead, I guess."

"They're very quick," Lucy commented several minutes later. It was moonlight again and they had a clear view of the men lowering something from the roof. Then they carried it along the path where they were hidden by the yew trees. Very slight sounds suggested they were putting it in the pick-up.

"They're very quiet too," Mark said. "Seems to me they've had plenty of practice. I bet they've stolen an awful lot of this stuff."

The three men came back into sight and stood at thc foot of the ladder. One of them began to climb and then stopped to say something.

"As soon as they're up on the roof again," Mark whispered, "and when the moon's gone in again, we'll creep away and ring the police. We've seen them at it and there's some of the stuff in their truck, that's all we need."

Yap, yap, yap! The shrill bark coming from the path sounded doubly loud in the silence.

Lucy was struck dumb with horror. Then she said, "It's Locket. She's got out and followed me. She'll come here to me."

"We'll have to bolt," Mark said at once, and he looked round for the best way.

It was plain that the men were alarmed and angry. Oaths reached the ears of Mark and Lucy. One of the men advanced down the path swearing that he'd do for the little something-or-other.

Lucy imagined a blow from a hammer or a hard kick on tiny Locket. "He'll hurt her," she cried.

"She may go back," Mark said. If he made a row and drew the men away Lucy could get away with Locket.

"She won't." Lucy knew Locket's courage. "She'll come to find me." She burst out into the open and ran along under the wall calling to Locket.

"Carry on, Lucy," Mark shouted and began to run towards the man on the path who stopped and swung round to meet him. The other two came down the path and Mark heard, "It's only a kid. Get hold of 'im."

Mark swerved away across the churchyard. Locket was quiet now and he thought they hadn't seen Lucy in the shadow of the wall. He dodged round a big tombstone and raced down a narrow path which led away from the church.

He wasn't worrying for he was a good runner—he had won some prizes and cups at his school sports for races of varying distances—and the path must lead to a gate so there was no danger of being cornered. Just lead them away so that Lucy could get back to the caravan, with that wretched little Locket, then he'd double round and join her. Ring the police as soon as the gang left.

The footsteps padding behind him sounded wrong, somehow, so Mark shot a glance over his shoulder. Only one of them. They'd gone after Lucy.

Lucy, racing along in the shadow of the high wall, was wondering anxiously if she'd find the lych-gate in the darkness. And where was Locket?

The lych-gate must be over to the right but the pick-up was in the road outside the gate and the men might be by it. She stopped to listen. There was a sound of running feet but they weren't coming towards her. It must be Mark. Good for him!

A cold little nose and scratching paws. *Locket!* Lucy scooped her up and tucked her under her arm. "Locket darling, don't bark now."

She crept forward keeping the yew trees between her and the path. There was a light cloud over the moon so it was fairly light. Her sandals made no sound on the grass. Near the gate she stopped and peeped through the lower branches of a yew.

The lych-gate, with its little roof, stood out against the sky. Beyond it the pick-up's windscreen shone dully and beside it there was a dark figure. The moon shone out and Lucy recognized him by his black leather jacket as the youth who'd wanted Locket.

She held her Yorkie a little more securely and turned away. There was no getting out that way. She began to move back towards the wall, hoping to find a place where she could climb over, not easy with Locket but—a dry stick cracked under her foot and she froze to stillness, her heart seemed to come into her mouth.

"Wha' zat?" came from behind her.

"Someone been watchin' us," another voice said. "I'd jes' like to know how long——" He broke off and Lucy heard heavy steps coming across the grass. She began to retreat towards the wall. If she circled round she'd find a way out. But where was Mark?

The footsteps came nearer, pounding down the path, and a breathless voice said, " 'E got awye. Let's get going. Quick."

The pick-up doors closed, and with a very little noise it moved off down the hill. Lucy heard the strange swishing sound of the wheels on the road as it gathered speed and then it faded away.

"Goodness!" she said out loud. "They're more frightened of us than we are of them!" She put Locket down and they both slipped through the shadows towards the gate. She'd only to run down the road and take the short cut to the forge and the safety of the caravan. It was very dark again but she found the gate. Something rustled under the tree beside her, bringing her heart into her mouth again, and she stopped.

"Okay," said Mark. "They've cleared out."

"Mark!" Lucy exclaimed thankfully. "Where were you?"

"I had a run round. I hoped they'd follow me but only one came, I lost him and then I slunk back."

They were out on the road now and the moon shone out again. Mark made for the telephone-box outside the little Post Office where the rows of groceries in the window seemed to be staring out at the silent street.

"Pity they got scared and bolted," Mark said, pulling open the door. "They may not go to the scrap yard but I'll tell the cops about it."

"I think they will, to get rid of the stuff they stole tonight," Lucy said, "and they can't know that we know about taking it there."

Mark dialled Police and gave a very brief account, which he had thought out beforehand, ending with the number of the pick-up. Then he replaced the receiver and came out into the road where Lucy waited.

"That's okay," he said. "Back to the caravan to wait for Deb and Jon."

CHAPTER TWELVE

MUFFLED HOOF-BEATS

IT WAS rather strange to ride almost noiselessly along the road, almost noiselessly but not quite, for in spite of their muffles the ponies made a subdued sound.

Like being somebody in a story, Debbie thought excitedly, and she tried to remember something she'd read about 'muffled hoof-beats'.

"Hear that?" Jonathan asked. "The phoney hoof noises. We only got away just in time."

In the night's stillness they heard the distant clop-clop down the village street. Debbie imagined people hearing it and keeping their heads under the bed-clothes until it had gone by; rather unkind to frighten them.

"It'd be fun if we could be ghosts and scare the chap doing it," Jonathan was saying.

"It's stopped," Debbie said. "I hope Lucy and Mark found a good place to hide. And I hope we do too," she added. "How far is it to the scrap yard?"

"Dunno exactly. 'Bout a mile," Jonathan replied vaguely. "Not far anyway. We turn to the right at the end of this long straight bit. It looks flat but it's still going down slightly and that pick-up can free-wheel almost all the way along here."

"Shall we trot?" Debbie suggested. They had to

get past the scrap yard and find somewhere to hide before the pick-up came.

"Okay." Jonathan let Kit-Kat go on, keeping him to a slow jog-trot. "Wonder how many loads they take in a night. I suppose they can't take very much at a time or it'd rattle and make the heck of a din."

They hadn't gone far before one of Puck's muffles wore through, and he sounded very odd indeed with only one hoof clinking on the road. Then one of Kit-Kat's muffles came off and Jonathan pulled up and got off to look at the others, which all needed tightening.

"We still don't make much noise," Debbie said as they rode on. "And it doesn't much matter now we're away from the village."

"We can't tell what may happen," Jonathan said and he looked over his shoulder. The moonlight showed the village with the dark mass of houses spreading up the hill and the church tower near the top. Were the gang at work therc now?

The moon became hidden again leaving them in darkness. They turned off the road up a narrow lane where the high hedges reached up into the darkness and branches of trees met overhead so that it was like riding into a tunnel.

As the sacking wore through the ponies made more and more noise. Jonathan said the ponies didn't want bits of sack flapping round their fetlocks, and they stopped to take it all off. They had to do this by feel and it took rather a long time

Debbie couldn't get rid of an uneasy feeling that

someone was coming after them, and when she got on Puck again she felt a little stab of fear as she heard a car start up in the direction of the road. It sounded alarmingly near. Jonathan heard it too.

"It's them," he said, "switching on the engine at the end of the hill. Why on earth are they so *soon*?"

"They'll see us," Debbie said frantically. "They're turning up this lane."

Jonathan said, "There's a gate here. Hurry!" He hadn't mounted Kit-Kat and he opened it and led his pony through with Debbie close behind.

"What luck finding it. Only just in time," she said as the lane was lit by the car's lights.

They stood behind the hedge while it passed. The gate was still open, but no one would notice that so long as the ponies kept still and quiet. Jonathan peered through the thick hedge as the car went by and said he was sure it was the pick-up.

"Who else could it be at this time of night?" Debbie asked. "I wish I knew why they'd got here so early."

"It's mucked things up," Jonathan complained. "Now we can't hide on the far side of the scrap place as we planned, and that means we can't go back the way we meant to."

"We can leave the ponies here," Debbie suggested, "and go and see what they're doing, if we can get near enough, but we can't find a place to hide and watch them from."

"Can't be helped," Jonathan said.

They tied the ponies to the gate and hoped for

the best because reins aren't very good for tying anything with, and though Puck would stand for hours Kit-Kat always became impatient and pawed and fidgeted.

Jonathan left the gate half-open so they could get through it quickly. Why quickly, Debbie wondered, as she slid her irons up the leathers, and remembered how he'd said anything might happen.

They went along the lane one behind another and walking very quietly. Jonathan went in front, he kept on the grass at the road-side which was in the shadow from the trees.

It seemed a long way to the scrap-dealer's yard and then, suddenly, there it was. They had come round a slight bend to where the road forked and, straight ahead, between the two roads, was a gate leading into the little triangle-shaped field full of scrap metal and junk.

Jonathan stopped dead and slowly sank down into a crouching position. Debbie copied him and they both stayed motionless in the deep shadow. The moon was shining again and the road ahead was light so that they could see the pick-up standing near the gate and the little group of men beside it.

Turning his head, Jonathan whispered softly, "Something must've gone wrong or they wouldn't be standing talking, and they got here rather soon. I'm going to try and hear what they're saying."

Debbie whispered back that Mark had said not to go close, but Jonathan crawled forward and she shrank back into the shadows to watch and wait. He was moving very slowly and cautiously—if only the beastly moon would go in again. As if in answer it did so and Jonathan became almost invisible to her.

The darkness was very welcome to Jonathan, for he'd just decided it wouldn't be safe to go any further, but now he was able to creep forward without going into a patch of moonlight. The men were all standing on the far side of the truck and he was able to make out what they were saying. He'd no plan, just to find out what was delaying them and what they'd do next, and then go back to tell Mark who'd tell the police.

"I'm fer goin' on," one voice said doggedly. "It was only a boy foolin' round. We needn't pack it in just fer 'im."

A match scraped and there was a little flare of light, then a whiff of cigarette smoke drifted to Jonathan.

"Yeh, but kids talk," another voice said uneasily.

"Let's get all we can and then clear out quick," suggested another.

A deeper voice asked, "Nothing to bring anyone here, is there?" They said there wasn't and they sounded satisfied about that.

"Fair enough," deep voice said, "clear out and lie low for a few nights. Start up agin if things seem quiet-like, see? And don't come hanging round here."

The scrap-dealer, Jonathan decided, and Mark must have scared them somehow and they'd got away. They said they'd unload what they'd brought and then get out. There was a general movement when this was settled. The gate was opened and the tail-board of the truck let down and one of them climbed into it.

"Cor!" he said. "Not a lot 'ere. Pity we 'ad to bolt wi'out a full load."

He began to pass something out and the other men carried it into the yard, they were gone several minutes before returning for more, and Jonathan saw the chance of carrying out a daring plan which he'd been turning over in his mind.

As soon as the three men had gone, laden, into the yard he began to crawl forward. One man was still in the truck, but it was facing Jonathan, so the roof of the front part hid him from the man. It was drawn up at the road-side with the driver's seat nearest the hedge. Jonathan reached the bonnet and edged his way along between the pick-up and the hedge. It was pitch-dark and the grass under his feet was soft. He moved slowly and silently. He was nearly at the door and he sighed with relief when he saw the window was open. As long as the moon didn't come out or the man in the back jump down——

His hand was feeling for the ignition key, as his fingers wandered over the dash-board he heard voices. They were coming back.

"That the lot?"

From the back of the truck a voice answered "Yeh."

Gosh, they'd drive away now, Jonathan thought in horror. He felt the key and snatched it, then he sank down on all fours. The man in the truck jumped down and Jonathan thought now one of them would come to the door to get into the driving seat and he began to crawl away. He felt very unprotected out on the road but he kept to the side where it was darkest and retreated as fast as was possible in a crouching position.

The pick-up door opened and then slammed shut. A minute later a voice asked angrily who'd got the flipping key? Several voices answered unintelligibly and Jonathan grinned as he went on crawling slowly, not risking putting on speed in case he was seen.

The moon treacherously emerged from a cloud for a brief instant, lighting up the road and showing up Jonathan quite clearly.

There was a yell. "Look there. Someone by that ditch."

"Another o' them kids. I'll——"

Jonathan didn't wait. He ran down the lane as fast as he could, shouting to Debbie to go. "Clear out, scram!" Footsteps were pounding after him but he had a start and he was a good sprinter. The moon, having done its worst, was behind clouds again and the lane was as dark as black velvet.

He reached the gate well ahead of his pursuer and found Debbie on Puck trying to pull the gate open wider. Kit-Kat flung up his head as Jonathan grabbed the reins and he found they'd come untied.

"Across the field, Deb," he said as he got the reins over Kit-Kat's head. He had his foot in the stirrup as the man came through the gate. It was a near thing! He let Kit-Kat follow Puck and pulled himself up into the saddle as they went along. Kit-Kat broke into his lovely smooth canter and Jonathan felt for the off-side iron. They were level with Puck and Debbie.

"Where are we going?" she asked. "It's so dark."

Then the moon obligingly came out and the field was lit with a silvery light. They saw that it was large, flat and bare of any obstacle. Kit-Kat was taking a hold and Jonathan let him go ahead as he liked to do.

Puck pounded along and Debbie was singing, "You can't catch me and Puck!" Glancing back Jonathan saw a figure standing at the gate and he couldn't resist letting out a yell of triumph. The excited ponies broke into a gallop and their riders let them have their heads. The cool night air fanned their cheeks and the ponies' hoof-beats thudded across the grass. Debbie didn't know that she was singing, she only knew she wanted to gallop on for ever. Then Jonathan was calling that they'd have to find a way out, Puck was slackening his speed and she was pulling up. They'd crossed the big meadow flat-out, now where were they to go?

"There's a gate," Jonathan pointed. "It goes into another field and we can work round till we get to the road again." And this is what they did.

"Call that breakfast?" Mark asked. "Looks like starvation!"

"It's all that's left," Lucy explained, "though cornflakes and tomato soup don't go very well together. There's a little marmalade left but I don't think——"

"Nor do I," said Mark.

"We'll be late at Mrs. Thursby's so we shan't get any lunch for ages," Jonathan said mournfully. "Pity we slept so late."

"I got enough milk for us to have tea," Lucy said. "And if Debbie hadn't 'phoned her zoo we could have bought some bread to eat with the marmalade."

"Sorry," Debbie said, "but I——"

"—— had to know how they were," Mark said teasingly. "Okay, we'll tighten our belts. Ajax and the ponies have plenty of feed left so they're all right."

They sat down to their strange meal, and though nobody ate much everyone talked a lot. Jonathan and Debbie told of their glorious gallop across the moonlit meadow and the exciting story of the ignition key. Their triumphant return to the village had coincided with the arrival of the police car, and there had been congratulations for them all when Jonathan handed the key over. It had been awfully late before they got to bed, but it had been terribly exciting and they felt it had been a very worth-while achievement.

"It was a wonderful night," Lucy said, after telling Jonathan and Debbie about Locket's escape (through a window as she had discovered later). "And the gang were scared of *us!*" she said in an unbelieving voice.

"I hope the cops caught them while they were trying to start the pick-up without the key," Mark said. "They'd find a way of starting it but it'd delay them."

It was then that visitors began to arrive. First

Mrs. Appleton, who looked at their plates in astonishment.

"That's no sort of a breakfast for growing children," she said.

"It's all we've got," Lucy explained, "because we've stayed away longer than we expected to."

"And it'll be all right because we're joining Mummie again today," said Debbie.

"Not without a proper breakfast inside you," Mrs. Appleton said firmly. "Wait you there, m'dears, and just warm your frying pan on that little stove." She hurried back to her cottage and quickly returned with a basket packed full—eggs, bacon, bread and butter. Soon they were eating a real breakfast.

"It's awfully good of you, Mrs. Appleton," Lucy said. They all tried to thank her but she wouldn't let them.

"No thanks, m'dears, not after what you done for our church. When I think of you out at night with the White Pony and those wicked men pretending to be it——" she said confusedly. "Well, 'tis done with, any road."

Then the Vicar arrived. He thanked them and praised them. "Such courage and resourcefulness—saving our church roof is something we'll not forget." They felt quite embarrassed.

He was carrying a large cardboard box, and Debbie, who had quick ears for anything of this sort, was sure she heard a faint rustling and scuffling from inside it.

"For you," the Vicar said, seeing her looking at it. He raised a corner of the lid and she peeped in.

"An owl!"

"Yes, a young one that fell out of the nest. One of my bell-ringers showed it to me this morning and asked for advice about it. I thought of you at once."

He beamed at Debbie and she beamed back at him.

"Thank you awfully. I'd love to have it. Tim Bristow is good at rearing young birds and he'll help me."

When the Vicar had left Mrs. Appleton helped the girls clear away breakfast while the boys fetched Ajax and the ponies.

"What'll you call your owl?" Lucy asked.

Debbie considered. "It's very pretty with those speckly fawn feathers. Speckles? I know, Spooky, after last night."

"Jolly good," Lucy said, "owls are spooky sort of things swooping about silently at night."

It seemed as if half Kensleigh turned out to see them leave and to wave good-bye to Debbie and Jonathan on the ponies, Lucy driving with Locket beside her and Mark walking with Tiger. They felt quite famous!

"A marvellous end to our holiday," Debbie said to Lucy as she rode beside the caravan. "And it's not quite the end." It would be fun telling her mother about the Mystery Pony, and then there'd be the fun of seeing her animals again.

"I can cross lots of days off my calendar," Lucy said. "And you know Deb, I feel so frightfully fit I'm sure the doctor will say I'm miles stronger when I go for my check-up."

And this really did happen, in fact Lucy was riding again before the year was up. Caravanning, they decided, was good for them.